THE POACHER'S GUN

THE POACHER'S GUN

By

William Wasserman

Copyright © July 2025 by Penn's Woods Publications LLC

All rights reserved. This book or parts thereof must not be reproduced in any form without permission in writing from the publisher. For information, address Penn's Woods Publications LLC, 38 Ganibrille Court, Simpsonville, SC 29681

ISBN: 979-8-218-67236-2

While these stories are based on actual events, I admit to taking substantial creative liberties and re-creating dialogue, places, businesses, and events. Except for some game wardens, I have given the characters fictitious names and have altered their physical descriptions. Any resemblance to actual persons, living or dead, businesses, companies, or events is entirely coincidental.

ALSO BY WILLIAM WASSERMAN

Poacher's Moon

Poacher Justice

Poachers, Lies and Alibis

Poacher Hunter

It's a Wild Life

Track of the Poacher

Wildlife Guardian

Game Warden

Poacher Wars

More Pennsylvania Wildlife Tails

Pennsylvania Wildlife Tails

The Best of It's a Wild Life

Trapping Secrets

Beaver Trapping and Snaring Methods

Muskrat and Mink Trapping

For Kathleen and Susie

All truths are easy to understand once they are discovered; the point is to discover them.
    ~ Galileo Galilei

x

Oh, Maggie, I wished I'd never seen your face
You made a first-class fool out of me
I'm as blind as a fool can be
    ~Song by Rod Stewart

THE OUTLAW COP

IT WAS BUCK SEASON back in the late sixties when Pennsylvania Game Warden Ed Bond had his first run-in with The Outlaw. In those days, many townships in rural Lehigh County had but one part-time cop. Bond enjoyed an excellent relationship with all police officers in his district, especially the state troopers. Many were hunters. They were honest, hardworking, and dedicated officers with strong moral principles who would never consider killing a deer during closed season.

All but one, that is.

He was an outlaw with a badge, and Ed Bond had been getting tips about his deer poaching activities for many years. But the tips were always too little or too late, and those few informants with solid information refused to testify against him in court. After all, the poacher was a cop, and they feared retribution if they presented testimony before a judge.

But things began to change when Ed's newly appointed deputy approached a hunter walking along a dirt road bordering a heavily posted wooded area.

The deputy wore a state-issued green Game Commission uniform and a badged Stetson hat, so there was no question regarding his authority when he asked to check the man's hunting license.

"What for?" the hunter grunted. "I'm just taking a walk."

The deputy was taken aback. A lanky young man in his late twenties, he'd checked a dozen hunters that morning—some with nice trophy bucks—and everyone had complied. It was obvious that the man was not merely taking a walk. Dressed in a bright orange hunting coat and ball cap, he cradled a scoped Model 70 Winchester rifle in his arms, and he was in an area known for its heavy population of whitetail deer.

"It's just a routine license check," the deputy said. "I work for Ed Bond. He asked me to patrol this area today."

The hunter stepped forward until he was only an arm's length away. Tall and broad-shouldered with cold gray eyes, he towered over the younger man. "So you're just doing what you were told, huh?" he said.

"That's right."

"Like I told you, I'm not hunting. I don't have to show you anything."

The deputy stepped back. In his first year on the job, he was unsure how to respond. Suspecting that the hunter was using a borrowed license or had already tagged a deer, he summoned the courage to press on (during that time, hunters were required to display their hunting license on the center of their back).

"If you don't turn around so I can see your license I'll have no choice but to arrest you for resisting inspection," the deputy said.

*"You...*are gonna arrest *me?"* the hunter scoffed. "Do you have any idea who I am?"

"That's why I want to see your license—to see who you are and if you're lawfully hunting."

The hunter poked a heavy index finger into the deputy's narrow chest. "I'm a police officer in this township, pal. Now get out of my way before *I* arrest *you!*"

With that, the hunter spun on his heels and started back down the road in the direction from which he had come.

Seeing a hunting license pinned to the man's coat, the deputy pulled a notepad and pen from his jacket pocket and scribbled down the number inscribed on its face. He noticed the turkey tag was attached to the lower corner of the license; however, the big game tag, which should have been directly above it, was missing. Pennsylvania allowed one antlered deer per season in those days but a few always chose to continue hunting after harvesting a legal buck. The deputy had no doubt that this man had planned to do exactly that.

Hunting license with the big game tag missing.

Alone and in a remote area with no immediate backup, the deputy let the hunter go on his way. He had identified himself as a local police officer, and if true, it would be easy to find him later. The deputy had a hunting license number, which would assist in identifying the man for prosecution of his game law violations later.

The deputy hiked back to his truck parked along the main highway, slid inside, and used his mobile radio to call Ed Bond and report the incident. Ed instructed him to patrol the immediate area by vehicle to see if he could locate the hunter again but not to approach him until he arrived at the scene.

Ed had been patrolling the southern end of his three-hundred-square-mile district and made a quick turnaround to head toward the center of the county. Traffic was heavy in his densely populated district and it took him half an hour to reach his deputy parked near the wooded area where he'd first confronted the hunter.

Ed pulled his marked patrol car broadside to his deputy's pickup and motioned for him to climb inside. The deputy jumped out of his truck and opened the passenger door and sat beside him.

"Find anything?" Ed asked.

He explained that he had searched the immediate area and discovered tire impressions from a vehicle, likely a pickup truck based on the tire size, which had been parked just off the road in a soft grassy patch. Fresh mud splattered across the road indicated the vehicle had left in a hurry.

"Think that was our man?" Ed asked.

"Without a doubt," the deputy said. "He claimed he was a police officer. Sure didn't act like one."

Determined to catch him, Ed used his mobile radio to call the Game Commission Regional office in Reading and have the dispatcher run the string of numbers on the hunting license that his deputy had noted. Minutes later, they were informed that the license belonged to Robert Lawless.

"Nice work!" Ed told the deputy. "We finally got him."

"You know the guy?"

"He's a career poacher," Ed said. "And just like he told you, he's a cop. I've been after him for years but it's like chasing a ghost."

"Should we keep looking for him?"

"No. He's too smart for that. Probably quit hunting for the day."

"What then?"

"Judge Cahill's office is close by. We'll head over there and I'll file charges against him."

Judge Cahill looked up unexpectedly as two game wardens pushed open a heavy glass door and walked into his reception room. In his mid-sixties, he had salt-and-pepper hair parted in the middle, dense white eyebrows, and light blue eyes that always gave the impression he was in a good mood. But not today. His secretary, Janie, was sick with the flu, which meant the judge was stuck answering phone calls and dealing with the mundane office duties she always handled for him.

"Well, speak of the angels and they appear!" chimed the judge as he stood from an ancient but well-kept wooden desk where he'd been sorting through a stack of legal documents.

Ed and his deputy exchanged curious glances.

"I just got off the phone with Robert Lawless," he said, focusing on Ed as he stepped around his desk and approached the wardens. "Seems he had a problem with one of your deputies."

"He had a problem because my deputy was doing his job," Ed said. "Lawless was hunting without a deer tag and refused to let my deputy check his license or see any identification."

"That's certainly not the story I got from him," the judge replied.

"My deputy is standing right next to me," Ed said. "Why don't you ask him about it?"

"Wish I could but I can't."

"Why not?"

"Because Lawless is going to file charges against your deputy for simple assault and harassment. As the judge who will preside over the hearing, I cannot discuss the circumstances beforehand with you or your deputy."

"He's lying, judge," Ed said. "My deputy did no such thing. In fact, we came here to file charges against Lawless for two game law violations."

"He's a cop, Ed. What are you talking about?"

"He's supposed to be enforcing the law, judge, not breaking it. It's buck season, and Lawless was out hunting when my deputy asked to see his license. Lawless got in his face over it and refused to cooperate. Then he turned around and walked away. He deserves to be prosecuted and that's exactly what I intend to do."

Judge Cahill pursed his lips and nodded thoughtfully. "That does complicate things now doesn't it," he said as much to himself as to Ed. Then he turned and went back to his desk and slowly lowered himself into a well-upholstered leather chair.

Ed and his deputy stood in silence as the judge drummed his fingers on the desktop while considering his options. After a long moment, his face lit up.

"Tell you what," he said, slapping both hands on his desk in an expression of finality. "I'll dismiss all the charges. Yours and his. Make this whole thing go away."

Ed shook his head from side to side. "I don't want you to do that, judge."

"It's not up to you," the judge said.

"Understood, sir. But my deputy didn't do anything wrong. Lawless is a police officer. He shouldn't be violating any laws, including game laws. I've been getting complaints about him for years. This is not an isolated incident; he's a poacher and he needs to be stopped."

The judge studied Ed's face for a long moment. "Your mind is made up, isn't it.

"Yes, sir."

"He's a cop," the judge cautioned. "There could be consequences for you and your deputy."

"I can handle that. I'm just asking you not to dismiss any of the charges I file against Lawless."

Judge Cahill leaned back in his chair and laced his fingers together as he considered Ed's request.

After a moment, he said, "I can grant you both a change of venue. I usually don't do that but I've known you for years, Ed, and I believe you're convinced you're doing the right thing. Besides, I don't want this case in my court. Lawless works in my township. Judge Richardson is a big-time hunter. He might be receptive to hearing the case. I'll call him later today. If he agrees, I'll set it up."

Judge Samuel Richardson was the physical opposite of wiry Judge Cahill. Short, squat, and obese, his black judge's robe bulged over a swollen belly and fell loosely around his thick ankles as he shuffled across the courtroom floor to his desk in slow, deliberate steps. He eased himself into a plush leather chair behind an oversized mahogany desk without looking up. If he had, he would have noticed Game Warden Ed Bond and his deputy, along with Robert Lawless, who were seated in front of him in padded metal folding chairs fifteen feet away. Lawless sat to the judge's right, the wardens to his left. There were no lawyers present.

Judge Richardson stared down at his desktop and examined the citations that had been filed in his office by both Bond and Lawless. After a minute, he slowly raised his eyes. His head was round as a hubcap with bulldog jowls that hung loosely below a thick, protruding chin. Clean-shaven, he had a full head of glossy black hair combed back. His movements were slow but his dark eyes were sharp and discerning as they flicked between the deputy and the cop.

"Someone here is lying and I aim to find out just who that person is," he said flatly. "It seems that we have a police officer who claims a deputy game warden assaulted and harassed him, and a deputy who claims a police officer resisted inspection and was hunting with an invalid license. Did I get that about right, gentlemen?"

Both Lawless and the deputy nodded their heads in unison.

"Good! I want to hear from the Game Commission first," the judge said. "Raise your right hand, deputy."

He did as he was told.

"Do you swear to tell the truth, the whole truth, and nothing but the truth?"

"I do."

"Have at it," the judge said as he leaned back in his chair.

Ed's deputy recounted what had happened several weeks prior when he had asked Lawless to produce a hunting license and he refused. His testimony was short but concise and lasted about ten minutes.

Next, the judge swore in Robert Lawless, who testified that Ed's deputy, while armed with a revolver plainly visible on his hip, had threatened to arrest him if he didn't show him his hunting license. Lawless claimed that because he wasn't hunting at the time, he was not legally bound to produce his license and that the deputy's antagonistic behavior constituted simple assault and harassment.

When Lawless finished speaking, the judge wrinkled his forehead and frowned. "And this is your testimony?" he asked, bemused.

Lawless looked both confused and somewhat surprised as he slowly nodded his head.

Judge Richardson leaned forward in his chair and narrowed his eyes. "Did the deputy, who was armed as you so distinctly made known to this court, point his gun at you?"

"No, but—"

"I'm not done yet," the judge said, cutting him off.

Lawless straightened in his chair.

"Did he remove it from his holster?"

"No."

"But you were brandishing a rifle at the time, weren't you? A scoped Model 70 Winchester, according to the deputy. Which, by the way, happens to be one of my favorite deer rifles."

"Yes, but—"

"I'm not done yet," the judge interrupted again.

Continuing, he asked. "You were dressed in a fluorescent orange coat and hat at the time, correct?"

"Yes."

"Why so, if you were merely taking a walk as you've testified?"

"So I'd be seen by anyone hunting in the area. I didn't want to get shot, judge."

The judge said, "I might accept that if your orange coat didn't have a hunting license pinned to its back. But it did, didn't it?"

Lawless gave a half-shrug. "Guess I forgot to take it off when I left the house. But that doesn't mean I was hunting, judge."

"Then why were you carrying a rifle during deer season if you weren't hunting?"

"Protection."

"Protection!" the judge said mockingly. "I didn't realize the deer were armed these days."

Lawless stared back at the judge in silence.

"What do you take me for, some kind of a fool?" the judge boomed, his ample cheeks bright red. "I've been a hunter all my life. I know exactly what you were up to, *Officer* Lawless, and I want you to know that you are a disgrace to your badge. You can count your blessings that you don't patrol in my township because after today, I would never believe anything you said in my court, and any defendant you brought before me would be found not guilty. Speaking of which, I hereby find *you* guilty of the charges filed against you and set the fine at five hundred dollars."

Judge Richardson turned to Ed's deputy, his demeanor softening. "And I find you not guilty, young man. And don't let this poor excuse for a police officer deter you from doing your job in the future. You did well. Keep up the good work. I've known Officer Bond for many years, and you're fortunate to be under his wing."

The judge picked up a wooden gavel lying on his mahogany desk and rapped it once against the hardened surface. "Court adjourned!" he declared. "The game wardens are excused, but Mr. Lawless shall remain seated until he makes arrangements to pay his fine."

Several years passed before Ed Bond had another run-in with Robert Lawless. During that period, he received numerous calls concerning the outlaw's poaching activities, but the information was always too sketchy or too late, and the informants always refused to testify for fear of retribution from the police officer.

But one day, his luck changed when he received a phone call from a woman named Maggie May, who claimed that Robert Lawless was hunting deer on his uncle's farm. Deer season was closed, and in a honey-coated Southern drawl, she said that Lawless was always bragging about how many illegal deer he killed and that she never wanted to hear about it again. She sounded more than a little upset.

Ed asked her for his uncle's name. Maggie told him it was Gerald Renner.

"Perry Township, right?" Ed asked.

"Yes, sir," she said. "Do you know him?"

"It's one of the farms where I stock pheasants every year. I know the property but I don't know Mr. Renner personally."

"Mercy me," she breathed. "I've heard all about those darling pheasants. Y'all might want to think twice about putting them there because right after you leave, Robbie's uncle calls him and he hustles over and shoots every one of them."

Ed felt the hair on the back of his neck stand up. Pheasant hunters were only allowed two birds per day.

"I really don't take much to hunting," Maggie continued, "but what Robbie does goes way beyond shooting a deer and bringing it home for the family. It's like an addiction with him. He can't stop himself."

"Can I ask why you're telling me this?"

Maggie paused for a moment. Then: "Guess it doesn't matter much who all knows at this point," she said. "I've been dating Robbie for over a year and I just found out that that two-timer is seeing another woman. He doesn't know that I know about her. But after today, it's over between us." There was both anger and despair in her voice.

"I'm sorry to hear that," Ed said.

"Bless your heart, sir," she purred, "but I'll be better off without him, anyway.

Ed said, "I'll head over to Renner's farm this afternoon but don't worry, I won't tell anyone where I got the information."

"Y'all won't have to," she said. "They'll know."

Gerald Renner walked out of his red, timber-frame barn and waved as Ed Bond parked his marked patrol car under an oak tree by the house and swung out of the vehicle. Ed was dressed in his green Game Commission uniform, including his badged Stetson hat. It was mid-October, and a blanket of tortured orange and yellow leaves crunched under his feet as he walked over to Renner under a darkening gray sky. They shook hands.

"Did you bring me more pheasants?" Renner asked with a forced smile. "The hunters cleaned them out since you were here last." Tall and in his mid-sixties, his face was lined with concern at Ed's presence.

"Not this time," Ed told him. What he didn't tell him was there would never be more pheasants now that he knew what was happening to them.

Renner stuffed his calloused hands into the pockets of his overalls and frowned. "What can I do for you, then?"

"Was Robert Lawless hunting here today?" Ed asked.

Renner stared at Ed for a moment, then nodded that he was.

Ed said, "I have good information that he killed a buck on your farm."

Renner winced at the news. "Who told you that?"

"I'm not at liberty to say."

"I don't know anything about a deer," Renner said. "Robert told me he was going after squirrels and pheasants when he showed up this morning. He left hours ago."

"Do you mind if I take a look around?"

Renner shrugged, sidestepped past Ed and started walking toward his house. "Go ahead and look," he said over his shoulder. "I'll be inside having dinner."

The farm consisted of roughly one hundred acres with half planted in unharvested standing corn. Ed walked along the edge of the cornfield and soon came upon a thin trail of blood mingled with scuff marks on the leafy ground cover. He followed the blood into a wooded area at the back of the property and soon came upon the entrails of a freshly killed deer.

Realizing he had solid evidence that a deer had been killed in closed season, Ed started back toward Renner's house to speak with him about his findings. When he reached the barn, he pulled a small flashlight from his jacket pocket and shined it inside the wide-open double doors. On the wooden steps leading up to the hayloft sat the head of a six-point buck, a thin trickle of blood staining the wood beneath it.

Gerald Renner had been watching Ed from the parted curtains of a kitchen window. As the warden approached, he opened the front door and stepped out.

Ed told him about the deer entrails he had discovered and asked about the head in his barn.

"I don't know anything about any of that," claimed Renner.

Certain Renner was lying, he pressed on. "The head puts you in possession of an unlawfully killed deer. It's a pretty stiff penalty."

"But I didn't put it there," Renner said.

"Somebody did," Ed said. "If it wasn't you, then who was it?"

Renner looked away and shrugged his shoulders.

"Possession of the head carries the same penalty as if you killed the deer yourself," Ed said. "If you don't tell me what's happening here, I'm going to prosecute you for having it in your barn."

Ed let that sink in for a moment, then said, "Look, Mr. Renner, I think we both know who did this, so why don't you end the charade? Tell me who killed the deer and I won't file any charges against you."

Renner rubbed the back of his neck and blew a long sigh. "Guess I got no choice," he said. "I'm not paying for someone else's mistakes, that's for sure. It was my nephew Robert, but you probably knew that all along."

"I had my suspicions," Ed said. "Now, where is the rest of the deer?"

"I don't know."

"I can get a search warrant and come back," Ed said. "If I find it, you will be charged."

"But it's not here," Renner insisted. "Robert took the deer with him. If you want to search my property, go right ahead. You don't need a warrant."

Ed believed him.

"What is he driving?" Ed asked.

"A black Ford F-150. Brand new, too."

"Did he take the deer back to his house?"

Renner paused and stared at Ed for a moment. There was the hint of a smile in his eyes.

"You know he's too smart for that, now don't you?" he said.

The sun had slid below the flat and treeless horizon as Ed Bond drove to Robert Lawless's house to see if his truck was there. When he arrived thirty minutes later, the lights were off and no vehicles were in the driveway. From there, Ed drove toward town, stopped at the first phone booth he came to and parked his patrol car. Hoping Maggie May would answer, he stepped inside the booth, closed the accordion doors behind him and dialed the number she'd given him earlier.

The phone rang twice and she picked up.

"Maggie, this is State Game Warden Ed Bond. Your information paid off. I found evidence of a freshly killed deer on the Renner farm, and his uncle admitted that Robert killed it earlier today."

"What's going to happen to Mr. Renner?" she asked with unease. "He's a sweet man. He always treated me like a lady."

"He won't be prosecuted," Ed replied. "He was cooperative. But the deer is gone and Robert isn't at his house. Do you have any idea where he might be?"

There was a short pause. Then: "You could try the Lumpkin farm on Hidden Valley Road since they're fine friends. Robbie goes elk hunting in Wyoming with Sam Lumpkin whenever they can draw a permit. Sam cuts up all of Robbie's deer for him, too. And he doesn't much care how many he kills."

Being familiar with the farm, Ed drove directly to it after hanging up with Maggie May. Hoping not to be spotted, he turned down the long gravel driveway toward Lumpkin's house with his headlights off. When he was halfway there, he saw Lawless's pickup truck parked under a pole lamp by the barn. Ed stopped his patrol car, shifted the transmission into park, and killed the engine. His dome light had been disconnected, so there would be no telltale glow when he eased open the driver's door and walked over to the truck for a look. There was a small pool of fresh blood and some deer droppings scattered on the floor of the bed. The droppings were dark, shiny, and wet. Still fresh.

Ed left his patrol car in place and started toward the house on foot. The lights were on inside, two yellow squares, and as Ed approached, he saw a form pass behind one of the curtained windows and quickly disappear. He froze, hoping he hadn't been spotted. Alone and in an isolated area at night, there was always the chance that someone might burst out of the front door armed with a shotgun and start blasting away.

After waiting for a long minute, he continued toward the house, thankful that the element of surprise would be in his favor. Catching a poacher off guard can be crucial at times. And a surprise visit from the game warden would put the odds in his favor. Ed was sure he had a solid case against Lawless, but he wanted an admission of guilt not only from Lawless but also from Sam Lumpkin if he'd been involved with the deer in any way. And one of the best ways to secure a confession is to confront the poacher by surprise before he's had a chance to conjure up some phony story or dispose of the evidence.

When Ed padded up three steps to the wood-planked porch, he saw a chest freezer sitting by the far corner of the house. Thinking some deer meat might be inside, he soft-shoed over to it and eased the lid open for a quick peek. The freezer was half full of frozen foods, much of it from a local grocery market, but there were also a dozen or more large packages wrapped in brown freezer paper that hadn't completely frozen. Each package had been labeled as deer meat with a heavy felt-tipped pen. Since the season was closed, the venison had to be from an illegal deer, most likely the buck that Lawson had killed earlier in the day.

As he moved toward the front door, Ed glanced into the window where he had seen someone pass by before. Sam Lumpkin and Robert Lawless sat at the kitchen table with a bottle of Jim Beam and two glasses of whiskey between them. He slipped past quickly so as not to be noticed.

Ed rapped on the wooden front door with his fist and waited. There was a pause, and he imagined both men staring at each other in dazed surprise. After a moment, he heard the scrape of a chair followed by heavy footfalls coming his way. He stepped back and off to the side as the door handle began to turn.

When the door swung open, Sam Lumpkin filled the frame wearing a white sleeveless T-shirt and tan canvas carpenter pants. He was broad-shouldered and clean-shaven with a square chin and slate gray hair trimmed into a buzz cut. Ed could smell the alcohol on his breath.

"Game warden!" Lumpkin croaked as he blocked the doorway. His eyes were wide with surprise in the moonlight.

"I guess you know why I'm here," Ed replied.

Lumpkin shook his head. "Nope," he said drunkenly. "I got no idea."

"I'm here about the deer."

"Deer! What deer?"

Ed couldn't help but chuckle inside. *What deer?* He'd heard it a hundred times before.

"The illegal buck deer you cut up for Robert Lawless," Ed said. "*That* deer."

Lumpkin let out a long roaring belch and wiped his thick lips with the back of his hand. Then he waggled a meaty finger in Ed's face. "You got no right coming onto my land and accusing me like that," he spluttered. "Game warden or not, I'm gonna punch you in the nose and throw you off my property."

Ed braced himself for a fight when Robert Lawless suddenly stepped behind Lumpkin and slapped a heavy hand on his shoulder. "You can't do that, Sam," he said. "He's a lawman. You'll get yourself into a pile of trouble."

Lumpkin spun around to face him. "But he—"

"No buts about it, Sam," Lawless said, cutting him off. "You need to get back in the house and let me handle this."

Lumpkin looked over his shoulder at Ed and back to the Outlaw Cop. "I still say he's got no right," he grunted. Then he brushed past Lawless and shuffled back into the house for another drink.

Robert Lawless stepped onto the porch and closed the door behind him. He looked sourly at Ed. "Maggie put you up to this, didn't she?"

Ed recalled her words when he said he wouldn't tell anyone about her.

Y'all won't have to. They'll know.

He ignored the accusation against Maggie. "I found fresh blood and deer droppings in your truck over there," he said. "Want to tell me about it?"

Lawless glanced over at his truck as if to confirm it was his. He paused for a moment. Then: "I picked up a roadkill on the way over here," he said. "Didn't want to let it go to waste."

Ed said, "So that would be in addition to the six-point buck you killed at your uncle's farm earlier today, right?"

Lawless looked stunned. "Don't tell me you were over there."

"I found the gut pile back in the woods and the head inside Renner's barn," Ed said. "Time to come clean, Robert."

"What's going to happen to my uncle?"

"Nothing, as long as you start telling the truth."

Lawless thought for a moment. Then: "It was no roadkill," he confessed. "I'll pay the fine. All I ask is that you keep my uncle out of this and that we do it on a field receipt. No citations."

Ed chinned toward the chest freezer he'd peeked into earlier. "Is that where you put the deer meat?" he asked, knowing it was.

"Yes," Lawless said. "There's about fifty pounds of it."

"Did Lumpkin cut it up for you?"

"Yes."

"He pays too, or there's no deal," Ed said. "He got his hands bloody and I'm going to charge him with the same penalty as you."

Lawless nodded that he understood.

"Start gathering up all the meat while I bring my patrol car over," Ed said. "It's evidence and it's coming with me."

One week later, Robert Lawless and Sam Lumpkin walked into the Pennsylvania State Police Barracks in Lehigh County and asked to see Ed Bond. Ed had made arrangements with the troopers to settle cases at the barracks when violators wanted to pay their fines through a written field acknowledgment of guilt rather than receive a citation or have a court trial. Because Robert Lawless was a cop, the last thing he wanted was to appear in court and risk being found guilty of poaching. He knew it wouldn't sit well with the County Commissioners or the people in the surrounding communities.

Ed had one of his deputies escort Sam Lumpkin to him first. The deputy, a six-foot-five barrel-chested man dressed in full uniform, ushered Lumpkin down a long corridor and stopped at an open doorway leading into a well-lit room at the rear of the barracks. Ed was sitting at a desk, waiting for them.

"Go ahead in," the deputy said in a deep bass voice. "I'll be waiting right here." His tone sounded like a warning, and it was meant to be.

Lumpkin strolled into the room like he owned the place. He walked over to Ed's desk and stood with his arms folded across his chest as he stared down at him with fire in his eyes. His chamois shirt and denim jeans fit tight across an athletic frame.

"Have a seat," Ed offered.

Sam Lumpkin slid back a wooden chair situated directly in front of the desk and sat heavily, his muscular arms still folded in an open display of contempt.

Ed slid a paper and ballpoint pen across the desktop toward Lumpkin. It was an acknowledgment of guilt form that illustrated the Game Law violation he'd been charged with. The fine was one hundred dollars.

This was in 1967. The fine would have a purchasing power of almost one thousand dollars today.

"Read it over and sign at the bottom," Ed told him. "I'm letting you off easy with only one charge for possession of an unlawfully killed deer."

Lumpkin picked up the pen and hastily scribbled his name on the line that indicated his confession. He reached into his shirt pocket, pulled out a hundred dollar bill, and slid the money back to Ed along with the document.

"I'm doing this in protest," he huffed. "I still think you were wrong."

"I'll give your money back right now if you'd rather take a hearing before a judge," Ed replied. "It's your call."

Lumpkin stood from his chair and shook his head from side to side. "Then you'd drag Robert into court. He doesn't want that."

Ed nodded in agreement. "I'd have no choice but to subpoena Robert and have him testify about what happened."

"Exactly. That's why I'm settling with you today and why I'm not going to have my attorney sue you for violating my constitutional rights."

He turned and started toward the door, then stopped halfway and spun around. "You came on my property without a warrant," he hissed. "That's trespassing. I won't forget that."

"I didn't need a warrant to knock on your door and talk to you," Ed told him. "Now, I think it's time for you to go."

The towering deputy who had escorted Lumpkin to the door stepped into the room and placed a massive open palm against Lumpkin's shoulder.

"Come with me," he rumbled, his deep voice filling the room. "I'll show you the way out."

Lumpkin opened his mouth to speak and the deputy tightened his grip. He thought better of it.

Robert Lawless stepped through the open doorway a few minutes after Sam Lumpkin had been escorted away. He sat in front of Ed Bond and fixed him with a cop's discerning eye.

"I know Sam's fine was a hundred dollars," he said. "That's a lot of money. I thought you might have gone a little easier on him."

"He's just as guilty as you are," Ed said. "And he has a bad attitude."

Lawless shrugged. "I guess," he said. "He's always been kind of a hothead."

Ed slid a field acknowledgment of guilt form and a pen across the table. "Sign at the bottom," he said. "But I want you to know that your penalty will be more severe than Lumpkin's."

Lawless narrowed his eyes. "What are you talking about? You told me to bring a hundred dollars, same as Sam."

"I'm not talking about the money."

"What then?"

"Closed season deer violations result in a three-year loss of hunting privileges. There will be six years in your case."

"Six years! Where did that come from?"

"You have prior arrests for game law violations," Ed said.

"You mean the run-in with your deputy a few years ago? I paid my fine for that. I thought it was over."

"It is, but you were arrested in Berks County last winter for failure to tag a deer and failure to produce the head of a deer that you killed."

"But it was a legal buck. I swear it."

"Without the head, there was no proof of that and you know it. The game warden in Berks County is recommending three years for those violations as well."

"Man, you guys are rough."

"There's more," Ed said.

"More…?"

"I know about the pheasants I released on your uncle's farm. You shot every one of them before the season opened. Unfortunately, I don't have enough evidence to prosecute you."

Lawless scowled with disgust. "Maggie told you about the pheasants, didn't she?" He spat out the words.

Ed looked at him and smiled. "No. You just did."

Three months later, Robert Lawless stood before the Board of Supervisors at a public meeting in the township he'd worked for as a police officer. The chief of police had fired him after the chief learned about his game law violations. In return, Lawless hired a high-priced Philadelphia attorney and appealed his dismissal to the Board, hoping they would override the chief's decision. Although Bond had considered going to the chief to report Lawless for his transgressions, he was concerned that the cop might cause trouble for Maggie May and had decided against it.

The Board had requested Ed's presence and he accepted. In addition to Ed, five township supervisors, the township solicitor, and the chief of police who had fired Lawless were in attendance.

Several dozen township residents were there as well. They sat on metal folding chairs in silent attendance, curious about a police officer working in their township who had been arrested by a state game warden for poaching deer.

The supervisors were seated side by side at a long table facing the spectators and announced the charges that had been filed against Lawless. They included killing a deer in closed season, failure to tag a deer that he shot in a state park, resisting inspection, and failure to produce the head of a deer to an officer of the Game Commission.

The supervisor was a longtime hunter, and after reading the charges, he asked Lawless what had ever possessed him, a sworn police officer, to go around violating game laws as if there were no consequences.

"Is this some kind of mental disorder?" he questioned. "If not, what kind of thinking would make you do these things?"

Lawless shrugged painfully. "I can't explain it," he said as he stood before them with his attorney. "I really don't know."

"That's all you have to say for yourself?" the supervisor asked incredulously.

Lawless nodded that it was.

Nathan Killjoy, Lawless's attorney, immediately spoke up, arguing that dismissal from the police department was far too severe considering that the game law violations he had been charged with were merely summary offenses in the Pennsylvania Crimes Code (a summary offense is considered to be a crime less serious than a misdemeanor or felony and can be heard in a magistrates' court without a jury). He suggested that a suspension without pay might be more appropriate if they were convinced that his client needed some sort of reprimand.

"I'm asking the Board of Supervisors to consider all of the good work that Roger has done for the people who live in this township," the attorney pleaded. "He is a conscientious police officer who has always done his best to keep the streets safe for every man, woman, and child who lives and works here."

"This man is a police officer!" the supervisor cried in rebuttal. "He is an official government representative who is not only required but *trusted* to work within the law—and that includes game laws! He must be held to a higher standard than the average citizen."

"Robert Lawless is a seasoned officer with years on the job," Killjoy shot back heatedly. "He's done a lot of good for the community. If the Board allows his dismissal to prevail, it would be a travesty. Furthermore, I promise to appeal the decision to the Lehigh County Court of Common Pleas at the taxpayers' expense."

"That's your prerogative," the supervisor said. "But it won't deter us from making the right decision. The public demands that the integrity of police officers must be above reproach."

The supervisor looked into the audience, his eyes searching for the chief of police, who was waiting to be summoned.

"I want to hear from Chief Trusty," the supervisor called out. "Chief, would you mind stepping up here for us, please?"

Benjamin Trusty stood in the back of the room dressed in his duty uniform, which consisted of a matching navy shirt and pants with permanent military creases in both, a black necktie, gold chest badge, polished black boots, and a leather gun belt holstered with a .357 Magnum Smith & Wesson Model 19 revolver. Trusty walked past the double row of spectators and stood in front of the Board of Supervisors.

"Chief, I want you to give us your reasons for firing Robert Lawless," the supervisor said.

Chief Trusty looked over at Lawless, who stood to his right with his lawyer, then turned back to the supervisor.

"First things first," he began, "I want to admit to the Board that my initial thought was to keep Robert on the force, punish him with a suspension and hope this whole thing would blow over. He was a good cop, except when he was hunting (there were muffled chuckles from the audience), and I wanted to give him a chance to straighten out. But after a lot of soul-searching, I realized that this man has no place in law enforcement. Cops cannot hold themselves above the law. And that is exactly what Robert Lawless had been doing for years. Keeping him on the job would have made me an accomplice as well. I had to let him go."

With his statement, Chief Trusty had sealed the Outlaw Cop's fate, and the meeting soon came to a conclusion with the Board of Supervisors confirming his dismissal and his attorney promising a prompt appeal to the county courthouse.

Ed Bond was about to slide into his patrol car parked behind the township building when Chief Trusty hustled toward him across the blacktop parking lot.

"Warden," he hollered. "Got a minute?"

Ed turned and waited for him to approach.

"I just wanted to congratulate you on your efforts in bringing a bad cop to justice," the chief said as they shook hands.

"Wasn't something I enjoyed," Ed assured him.

"Makes two of us," the chief agreed. "But like I said inside, once I found out about the violations, I had to let him go."

"Mind if I ask how you heard?"

"It all started with an anonymous phone call," the chief said. "Same way a lot of crimes are solved. Only this time, the bad guy was one of our own."

"Let me guess," Ed offered with a shrewd smile. "A woman with a sweet Southern accent."

"That's right. Did she call you, too?"

"Sure did," Ed replied. "And you know what they say about a woman scorned."

Author's Note

As promised, Robert Lawless appealed his dismissal to the county courthouse. The court upheld his removal from the police force.

Tell me do you think I'm dumb?
Talking 'round in circles with your tongue
But I know you lie
'Cause your lips are moving
      ~Song by Meghan Trainor

THE KEEPER'S CLOSET

HE HAD BEEN dumping bags of bright yellow shelled corn in his back yard for weeks on end. Just below the upstairs bedroom window, it made for a perfect shot. There were no homes behind his place, just a sea of snow-covered fields spilling into a large tract of woods, and nobody was on either side of him. Somewhat isolated, with the nearest neighbors several hundred yards away and across the road, he felt perfectly safe as he eased open the bedroom window and leveled the crosshairs of his .30-30 Winchester behind the buck's front shoulder.

Kapow!

It was a solid hit and the six-pointer sprang straight up, then sprinted off with its tail tucked between its legs.

But that's when things started to go wrong. The deer was supposed to drop dead in its tracks or maybe run a short distance before collapsing in the field behind his house. Instead, it spun around and bolted through his front yard and across the township road, only to disappear into a broad tract of woods.

It had been a good shot. Of that, he was certain. The deer wouldn't get far. But there were several homes on the other side of the woods. And it was Sunday. Hunting was not allowed. What if somebody heard the shot and decided to look around? What if they found the deer? They could follow its tracks right back to his house with the recent snowfall.

But it was early morning and he figured most folks would still be in bed. So, with that encouraging thought in mind, he grabbed his coat off the floor and ran down the steps and out the front door, hoping to retrieve the deer before anyone saw him.

He could see rooftops in the distance as he crossed the township road and made his way through the open woods under a heavy white sky. He leaped over old fallen logs and weaved quickly through the naked trees as he followed the buck's bloodied tracks through the snow. But the deer had managed to get farther than he thought it would, and when he reached the woods' edge and saw it lying dead on the front lawn of someone's house, his chest tightened with dread.

A thin line of smoke curled from the chimney as he slipped behind a tree and watched the house. Dawn was breaking and no lights were on inside, suggesting that the occupants were still asleep or not at home. And although the snow-covered sidewalk bordering the property was packed with footprints, not a soul was around.

It was now or never, he thought as he raced over to the deer and dropped to his knees in the snow. He pulled a razor-sharp folding knife from his pocket and quickly unzipped the carcass. Then he reached up into its warm chest cavity with the blade, cut through the windpipe, and pulled out the entrails while glancing over his shoulders like a thief in the night. Confident that no one was watching, he dropped the steaming gut pile in the snow and grabbed the buck by its bony antlers and quickly dragged its limp carcass back into the woods out of sight.

Pennsylvania Game Warden Jason Farabaugh was returning to his district in Fayette County after some time off when he received an anonymous tip about a suspected deer poaching incident. The information had been recorded on a *Turn-in-a-Poacher* hotline (a toll-free phone line for reporting game law violations) while he was away. Although it was his father's birthday and he had planned to see him today, time was of the essence. Jason felt it was necessary to look into the tip about the deer first.

The informant stated that he'd seen a freshly killed deer lying in someone's front yard while walking to church. Thinking it was a roadkill, he paid it little mind, but on his way back home he noted that the deer was gone and observed a swath through the snow indicating that it had been dragged into the woods. He gave the street address where the incident had occurred and hung up.

But that was two days ago and several additional inches of snow had fallen since the tip had been reported, the fresh powder obscuring any plainly visible evidence as Jason arrived on the scene. Still, he could see a faint depression in the snow leading from the yard where the deer had been found into a wooded area. Jason followed the imprint, hoping it would lead him to the deer, but it ended abruptly just inside the tree line as if the animal had suddenly vanished.

There were several faded sets of boot prints in the snow at the edge of the woods. One set led deeper into the timber. He followed those tracks for a considerable distance until they took him up a steep embankment. When he reached the top, he scanned the landscape below. A two-story wood frame house stood at the edge of a road a short distance ahead. The tracks led toward it, so Jason continued on until he reached the road. The house was on the opposite side, and he could see a man in the back yard dressed in a red plaid shirt and brown canvas hunting pants. He appeared to be frantically searching for something, but when he suddenly looked up and saw the warden dressed in full uniform, he quickly retreated into the house.

Jason hurried across the road, vaulted up on the front porch, and knocked on the door.

No response.

Drops of dried blood were on the wooden floorboards by the door and the tracks he'd been following led to the house. The blood had to be from the illegal deer, he thought.

He knocked again, louder this time.

Still, no response.

Having no intention of leaving without answers and knowing someone was home, he hammered on the door with his fist.

"Hold your horses!" came a raspy cry from inside. After a moment, a woman swung open the door, her heavy frame filling the entryway. In her mid-forties, she had brown hair pulled back tight to her head, a fleshy face, and dark questioning eyes. She wore a gray woolen sweater over faded jeans and tan work boots.

"Game warden!" she croaked in surprise. "Can I help you?"

"I'd like to speak with the man I saw in your back yard a minute ago," Jason said. "He was wearing a red shirt."

The woman eyed him severely and for a moment, Jason thought she might slam the door in his face.

"That'd be my husband," she said. "What's he done this time?"

"Not sure I know," Jason replied. "But I have a few questions I'd like to ask him about a dead deer."

She gave the warden a look that said she wasn't surprised. Then she turned her head and hollered into the house.

"*TOMMMEEEEEE!* You'd best come out here. Somebody wants to talk to you."

Tall, thin, and gaunt, with three days of stubble and a mop of greasy hair hanging in his face, Tommy looked to be about the same age as his wife.

"Can I help you?" he asked Jason as if surprised to see him.

Jason noticed his breathing was heavy, like he'd just finished a workout.

"I'm with the Pennsylvania Game Commission," Jason said. "You could start by explaining where the blood on your porch came from."

Tommy looked down at the crimson stains and shrugged. "A buddy of mine brought me a deer last week," he said. "He killed it legal during deer season if that's what you're here for. He asked if I would help him cut it up, so I did."

"Mind if I come inside and take a look around?" Jason asked.

"Not at all," Tommy replied. "You're welcome to look in my freezer, too."

When Jason stepped into the house, he was surprised to see a skinning gambrel hanging from the ceiling in an unfurnished dining room to the left of the doorway. A fresh deer leg lay on the bare hardwood floor beneath it.

Clothes, toys, and assorted junk were strewn all over the floor along with the leg, creating an obstacle course for Jason or anyone else daring enough to enter the house. Piles of dishes could be seen overflowing the sink in the next room, and the air was thick with the musty smell of mildew and stale food.

Jason looked down at the severed leg and back to Tommy. "Where's the rest of the carcass?"

"My buddy came and got it," Tommy said.

"The same buddy that brought you the deer?"

"Yep."

"What's your buddy's name?"

Tommy hesitated, then shook his head. "I don't know," he said.

Jason said, "So you want me to believe that you cut up a deer for a buddy of yours but you don't know his name. Is that about right?"

Tommy shoved his hands in his pockets and nodded a yes.

Shocker, Jason thought mockingly.

Convinced that Tommy was lying, Jason decided to get directly to the point.

"What can you tell me about the dead buck that was lying on someone's front lawn on the other side of the woods?" he asked.

Tommy and his wife exchanged nervous glances. "I don't know nothing about it," Tommy said.

"You sure about that?"

"Positive."

"Footprints in the snow led from the deer, through the woods, directly to your house," Jason said. "How do you explain that?"

"That don't mean they're mine. Lots of people walk around in them woods."

"But lots of people don't have a skinning gambrel in their house with a deer leg lying under it and blood on their front porch."

Tommy suddenly found his boots to be interesting and studied them in silence.

"Know what else lots of people don't have?" Jason said as he reached out with his right hand and picked a threadlike strand off Tommy's chest. "They don't have deer hair all over the front of their clothes."

"He never takes a bath!" his wife blurted out as Tommy frantically began to brush the hairs away with both hands in a vain attempt to shed the evidence.

Realizing it was useless, he stopped and looked at Jason. "I won't lie no more warden," he said wearily. "The deer is here all right. I got scared when I saw you from across the road, so

I ran inside and ripped it off the gambrel and carried it upstairs."

His wife rolled her eyes in disgust, apparently caught by surprise that the dead deer had been brought into their bedroom.

"Let's go get it," Jason said. "I'll give you a hand bringing it down."

Jason followed Tommy up a wooden stairway and down a long hallway. As they entered the bedroom, Jason couldn't believe his eyes when he saw the partially butchered deer lying in a closet, buried under a large pile of clothes and other household items. The bed had also been haphazardly pushed in front of the open closet door in a frantic effort to hide the carcass.

Jason had to suppress a chuckle when he saw one of the deer's front legs protruding straight up from behind the bed as if it were saying, "Hey, warden, I'm over here."

Tommy and Jason each took one end of the illegal buck and carried the carcass down the stairs and out the door to the front yard so Jason could pick it up later with his state-issued patrol vehicle.

After further questioning, Tommy admitted that he'd shot the deer from the bedroom window on a Sunday morning over a pile of shelled corn.

Later that week, Jason filed the appropriate charges against Tommy, including hunting on Sunday and hunting over bait. Tommy thought the penalty was too severe and decided to take a court hearing before the local district justice. In the end, he was found guilty of all charges, fined hundreds of dollars, and had his hunting privileges in Pennsylvania revoked for a lengthy period of time.

All game wardens recognize that there are no guaranteed days off in their line of work, especially when working from home, as most wardens do. And for Jason Farabaugh, a day he'd set aside to spend time with his father had been sidetracked by an anonymous poaching tip.

Fortunately, he was able to bring the case to a successful conclusion and keep his date with his dad later in the afternoon. The events of the day only adding to the birthday chat they had together.

O Christmas Tree, O Christmas tree,
How lovely are your branches!
Not only green in summer's heat,
But also winter's snow and sleet.
 ~Christmas Carol

A MATTER OF THEFT

THE GAME COMMISSION owns over a million acres of rural property in Pennsylvania called State Game Lands. These properties consist of woods, fields, streams, and lakes where the agency manages wildlife habitat to provide opportunities for lawful hunting, trapping, fishing, boating, horseback riding, and hiking. Although the lands are open to the public, removing or otherwise injuring plants, trees, and shrubs is a violation.

So, on December 22, 1963, when Land Manager Ed Flexer radioed Game Warden Ed Bond (called Game Protectors in those days) to report that three spruce trees about six feet tall had been taken from State Game Lands, Bond arranged to meet with him and look into the violation.

When Ed arrived at the scene, he saw drag marks in the snow littered with spruce needles where the trees had been brought from the woods out to the road after being cut with a chainsaw. Boot prints in the snow bearing two different tread patterns told him both thieves were likely adult men of equal size and weight. There were fresh tire tracks from their vehicle on the snow-covered road. Ed followed them on foot for a short distance, occasionally coming upon a small scattering of spruce needles centered in the road between the imprint of the tires.

The heavy scent of pine and spruce filled the air as Ed quickly walked back to his car and motioned for his partner to climb inside along with him. Thinking the thieves might live close by, he started his engine and followed their tracks down the winding country road, hoping they would lead them to their suspects.

It had snowed quite a bit over the past several weeks and because this was a rural and seldom-used road, it was barely wide enough for two cars to pass. But after being dug out by the county plow, with four-foot-high snowbanks on each side, it looked more like a winter bobsled trail as Ed followed their tracks all the way to the little village of Erwinna and up to the front door of an old Victorian house.

In those days, game wardens drove their personal vehicles and often did not wear uniforms, so when Ed and his partner knocked on the door and an elderly lady answered, she had no idea who they were.

"Can I help you, gentlemen?" she asked. A kindly woman with silver hair cut fashionably short, she smiled at them with crystal-blue eyes.

With the door open, both men could see she had been decorating a freshly cut spruce tree. After asking for directions as if they'd lost their way, Ed Bond lifted his gaze over her shoulder and said, "Oh my! What a lovely Christmas tree. Would you mind telling us where you got it?"

My son bought it for me," she beamed. "He's home now if you want to ask him about it. It's the fifth house down on your left. The nice red brick ranch."

"Thank you," Ed said. "We'll head over there right now."

She nodded, her eyes sparkling in the morning sun. "You're quite welcome. I'm Mrs. Justice. My son's name is James. I'm sure he'll be happy to help you."

As they turned and walked away, the woman sang out, "Merry Christmas, gentlemen!"

Ed's partner turned to him and muttered that he was beginning to feel like the Grinch who stole Christmas.

Ed nodded in agreement.

When they knocked on her son's door, a man in his early thirties answered. He had his mother's eyes.

Ed pulled back the bottom of his coat to expose a bright silver badge attached to his belt. "State game warden," he said. "We're here about the trees."

"What trees?" Justice replied. "I don't have any trees."

The response is always the same, Ed thought, *whether it's a deer or a tree.*

Sitting on the couch behind him was another man and a little boy about five years old, watching *Captain Kangaroo* on TV. When Justice said he didn't have any trees, the little guy turned his head toward them and cried, "Yes, we do, Daddy. It's our Christmas tree!"

James Justice looked over at his son and back to the wardens, his expression pained.

Ed had to stifle a smile, for he immediately thought of the popular TV show *Kids Say the Darndest Things*, hosted by Art Linkletter.

"Follow me," Justice said as he stepped outside and closed the door behind him. "It's around back."

Ed and his partner tailed Justice to an open shed attached to the back of the house, where they found a freshly cut spruce tree leaning against the back wall.

"Kids!" Justice said with a look of exasperation. "You never know what will come out of their mouths."

"Just being honest," Ed replied.

Justice shrugged. "Yeah, I guess."

"Nice tree," Ed said. "But you could have bought one just like it for about five bucks. Now you're looking at a twenty-five-dollar fine for this tree and another twenty-five for your mother's ($250 each in today's money)."

Justice winced. "You're kidding?"

"Afraid not."

"But there are thousands of them back in the woods. Nobody's going to miss them."

"My partner and I will miss them."

"But I didn't know they belonged to anybody," Justice whined.

"Everything belongs to somebody," Ed said. "Besides, the property is posted as State Game Lands. You can't miss the yellow signs."

Justice stuffed his hands in the back pockets of his jeans and shook his head. "Can't you give me a break?"

Ed regarded him for a moment before saying, "Mr. Justice, I'm being more than fair with you. You're facing a summary offense here, which means you won't have a criminal record. I could also charge you under the Crimes Code for larceny, which would be a misdemeanor leading to more serious consequences than merely paying a fine."

Justice nodded soberly. "Duly noted," he said. "It's my own fault, anyway."

"Where is the third tree?" Ed asked.

"Third? I only took two."

"There are three fresh stumps back in the Game Lands," Ed said. "Three spruce trees were taken."

"Must've been somebody that came after I left," Justice responded.

Ed thought it was possible that he was telling the truth and that someone else could have taken the third tree. After making arrangements with Justice to settle his violations on a field acknowledgment of guilt later in the week, Ed and his partner drove back toward the Game Lands to revisit the area where the trees were taken.

Halfway there, the thought occurred to Ed that the other man in the house watching TV with Justice's son might have taken the third tree. He made a three-point turn on the narrow road and drove back to Justice's home to interview the man, but he was gone.

"What do you want him for?" James Justice asked.

"I think you know," Bond replied, deadpan.

Justice crossed his arms and set his jaw. He said nothing.

"Cooperation goes a long way with me," Ed offered. "There's still that larceny charge I told you about. I'm sure you don't want that."

"You're right, I don't, but…"

"No buts. Where is he?"

Justice blew a heavy sigh and nodded to his right. "That's his house, next door. He's my brother, Ralph."

Ed and his partner went to the house and knocked on the front door. When no one answered, they walked around to the side of the house just in time to see Ralph Justice frantically shoveling snow on top of a spruce tree lying in his back yard. When he spotted the wardens, he dropped his shovel and strode toward them, calling an imaginary dog, and even asked them if they had seen it. The only problem was that a drag mark in the snow littered with Christmas decorations anyone could follow led from the back of his house right up to the tree.

Ed assumed his brother James had a guilt complex and quickly called to warn him that the wardens were coming. In a way, he couldn't blame him. After all, they were family.

Realizing that his ploy about a lost dog was not going to work and that he'd been caught red-handed, Ralph asked Ed what was going to happen to him.

Ed told him he would be fined for taking the tree and instructed him to leave it there and follow him back to his brother's house.

After they had all assembled in the living room, Ed explained that he had every right to confiscate all of the trees in addition to their fines.

The brothers both swallowed hard at the notion.

After a pause, Ed said, "Don't worry, we're not going back to your mother's house to take her tree. It would not only completely ruin her Christmas but would break her heart to know how her sons got it for her."

He looked directly at James Justice. "And we are not going to take your son's Christmas tree and ruin his day either."

"I appreciate that, really, officer," he replied.

"I just hope this is a lesson for both of you," Ed continued. "It makes no difference whether it's a wallet dropped on the sidewalk or a tree taken from the woods; if it doesn't belong to you, it's still a matter of theft."

I came, I saw, I conquered.
~Julius Caesar
Letter to the Roman Senate 47 BC

THE RULE OF THREE

THE FIRST TIME that Ed Bond encountered a member of the Skeever family was during the October archery deer season back in the mid-seventies. It all started when a deputy game warden on patrol observed a Dodge pickup truck parked in a wooded area. A brightly colored decal attached to the rear window referenced a local bowhunting club, so the deputy parked his car and stepped out to inspect the vehicle.

He examined the truck's bed and the area around the tailgate for blood and hair that might indicate a deer had been taken earlier in the season. Seeing nothing suspicious, he advanced to the cab and peered into the passenger window, where he observed a compound bow and quiver lying on the seat. Believing the hunter may have taken a deer and then returned to his truck to drop off his archery equipment before going back to retrieve the carcass, the deputy stood by and waited for him to appear with his kill.

It wasn't long before a man dressed in camouflage clothing emerged from the trees. In his fifties, he was lean with shifty eyes, a pinched face, and a long, crooked nose. He had no archery equipment with him and was limping uncomfortably on his right leg as though he had just injured himself.

Concerned for his welfare, the deputy asked if he was hurt.

"Who me?" he answered, looking left and right as though others were present.

"You're limping," the deputy said. "Thought you might be hurt."

"Nope. I'm fine."

"What's your name?"

"Slim Skeever."

"Is that your truck?" the deputy asked, chinning toward the Dodge.

Skeever looked at the truck, then back to the deputy. "Sure is," he said.

"Is that your archery equipment inside?"

"Yep," he replied. "But I'm not hunting; I'm just taking a walk."

His answer aroused suspicion. Why would someone so painfully awkward in his movements be hobbling around in the woods dressed in camouflage clothing? Why did he bring his archery equipment only to leave it in the truck? In fact, why bring it at all if he was only taking a walk? And if he wasn't injured, why was he limping so severely?

The deputy lowered his gaze to the man's legs and noticed that his jeans fit tightly over his right leg but hung loosely over his left. Looking closer, he suddenly realized why Skeever was limping.

"Lift up your right pant leg," the deputy ordered.

Slim Skeever started grinning like a pack mule eating briars. Then he hiked up his pant leg just enough to reveal the business end of a deer rifle pressed against his flesh. It was unlawful to be in possession of a firearm during archery season.

"Hard to believe you did that," the deputy said. "It's a good way to blow a hole in your foot."

Skeever shrugged and said nothing.

"Hand it over," the deputy directed.

Skeever loosened his leather waist belt and held up his pants with his left hand while reaching into his jeans with his right for the rifle.

"Nice and slow," the deputy cautioned, gripping his holstered revolver.

Skeever carefully extracted the rifle from his trousers and handed it to the deputy.

"You have a nice bow in your truck," the deputy said. "Why aren't you using it?"

"I'm a lousy shot," Skeever replied. "Bought it a few days ago and can't hit a thing with it."

"I'm not surprised," the deputy said. "A few days isn't long enough for most folks to learn how to shoot a bow accurately."

Skeever shrugged. "Guess not."

"The fine is one hundred dollars," the deputy said. You can settle on a field receipt or take a court hearing. Your choice."

"I'm guilty," Skeever said. "No sense going to court over it."

Thankful that his investigation had paid off, the deputy couldn't help but think that if the hunter had made up a story about tripping over a log and injuring his leg, he might have checked his hunting license and sent him on his way. The lever-action rifle had been well concealed and he might have missed it.

Slim Skeever met Ed Bond at the state police barracks later that week and paid his fine through a field acknowledgment of guilt (a system we used to have where someone could pay a fine to the game warden, thus avoiding a hearing before a judge and court costs). Still, Ed had been hearing rumors about the Skeever family and their poaching exploits for many years. He was certain they would meet again, and several years later, he had his second run-in with members of the clan.

The Skeever brothers were minutes away from their regular hunting spot as they drove along Route 413 when Moe

Skeever spotted the deer. Only seventy yards away, it stood alone in the open field at the edge of the woods. A perfect shot.

"Pull over, quick!" Moe cried, pointing at the deer through the windshield. "There's a nice one right there."

Joe Skeever glanced at the deer, then shifted his eyes to the sideview mirror before easing his red Ford pickup to the shoulder of the road, where he stopped. The blacktop highway was empty behind him.

"Coast is clear," he said. "Put it down quick."

Moe rolled down the passenger window and reached for the scoped rifle leaning against the seat between his knees. Shifting his weight, he slid sideways in the seat, pointed the barrel out the open window, and brought the wooden stock to his shoulder. The deer stood broadside to them and paid them no mind as it grazed on the tall grass at its feet.

Moe's rifle barked once and the deer leaped straight up then fell to the ground, its heart pulverized by the deadly missile.

"It'll be dark soon," Joe Skeever said with a hint of alarm. "Let's get her into the woods before somebody sees us."

Moe left his rifle on the seat as he shouldered open the door and leaped to the ground. His brother followed, both men slamming their doors shut and charging into the field.

It was buck season, and they had just killed an illegal doe.

But the Skeever family didn't care much about seasons and bag limits. They were career deer poachers who followed the motto, "If it's brown, it's down." They lived to hunt and hunted to live, primarily by eating wild fish and game that they killed whenever they pleased.

Each taking a front leg, the men quickly dragged the limp carcass fifty yards to a wooded area and slipped behind the trees where they wouldn't be seen from the road.

Joe drew his hunting knife from its leather sheath and opened the carcass from rectum to sternum with its razor-sharp blade. A gentle steam drifted into the cool evening air from the deer's open chest cavity. He reached deep into the rib cage, cut loose the entrails, and dumped them on the ground in a loose pile, the pungent odor of moist viscera filling their nostrils.

Joe breathed it in. "Ahhh, I love the smell of success," he said with a crooked grin.

"This ain't no time to gloat," Moe hissed. "We still gotta get this baby home and I don't like the idea of dragging it back to the truck when somebody might see us."

Headlights blinked through the trees from the highway. The sun had set and traffic had picked up considerably with the workday coming to an end.

"We'll leave it here and come back after midnight," Moe said. "Safer that way."

"Sounds like a plan," Joe said. "Now, let's head over to Tony's Tavern for a celebration drink. I'm getting thirsty."

Around noon that same day, Ed Bond had received a tip about a red Ford pickup truck parked along Route 413 near a wooded area daily for the past week. The informant had explained that the truck would stay until well after dark and that he expected late hunting.

Ed made it a point to head over to the location after sunset and had arranged for a deputy to accompany him. When they arrived, they saw a red Ford pickup parked along the road's shoulder, just as the informant had said.

Unbeknownst to the wardens, the Skeevers had just returned to their truck after hiding their illegal kill back in the woods. And as Ed Bond steered his patrol car toward the shoulder behind them, their headlights switched on. Ed hit the gas and whipped his vehicle around the truck, stopping in front of it and blocking their escape.

Moe sat by the passenger door; his eyes wide with surprise as the wardens lit him up with their Maglites. His brother, Joe, sat with both hands on the steering wheel, looking straight ahead as if he were driving.

The deputy moved to Moe Skeever, opened the passenger door and escorted him to the back of the truck while Ed rapped on Joe's window with his knuckles. "State game warden," he said, shining his light into the cab. "Step out of the truck."

Joe Skeever rolled down his window and squinted at the warden. "Why? I ain't done nothing wrong."

"There's a rifle on the seat next to you," Ed said. "Hunting after hours is a Game Law violation."

"But we weren't hunting late," Joe protested. "Moe and me was way back in the woods and it took us a while to walk out. That's all."

Ed shined his Maglite on Skeever's hands. They looked like he'd been working in a slaughterhouse for a week and hadn't washed them.

"Okay," Ed said. "Where's the deer?"

"What deer? I don't know what you're talking about."

Ed's deputy overheard the conversation and called out to him: "Hey, Ed," he hailed, "my new friend Moe and I are going to take a walk and look for the deer. Shouldn't take us too long."

"Go ahead," Ed called back. "I'll keep this one company."

Warden Bond looked hard at Skeever. "It's just a matter of time before my deputy finds it," he cautioned. "Do you want to talk?"

"Got nothing to say."

"Step out of the truck," Ed told him.

Skeever immediately tightened his grip on the steering wheel. His body stiffened.

In a matter-of-fact tone, Ed said to him, "If you refuse to cooperate, I'm going to use whatever force is necessary to remove you from the vehicle. It won't be pleasant and you might even be injured. Then I'm going to charge you with resisting inspection, put you in handcuffs, and take you straight to jail."

Turning off his 4-cell Maglite, Ed flipped it front to back and tapped a slow, methodical beat on the truck's door frame with its inch-and-a-quarter hardened aluminum tip. "Last chance," he said. "Take your hands off the steering wheel and step out of your vehicle."

Joe Skeever met the warden's gaze and knew he meant business. He started nodding like a woodpecker hammering for termites. "Okay," he moaned. "I don't want no trouble. I'm getting out now."

Skeever eased open his door and slid out of the truck. Ed handcuffed him and removed the rifle lying on the seat. After securing it inside his patrol car for evidence, he saw his deputy and Moe Skeever coming out of the darkened field with the illegal deer.

Moe Skeever was hunched forward, breathing in ragged gasps as he dragged the heavy carcass all by himself.

"You killed it," the deputy had told him. "Now you can haul it back."

When Ed Bond received notice that the Skeever brothers had requested a hearing in front of the local district justice, he was more than a little surprised. After all, they had both been caught red-handed—literally. Ed still had the rifle they'd used along with photos of the illegal deer, not to mention the fact that they had both admitted to killing it in front of him and his deputy that night.

Joe and Moe Skeever had each been charged with possessing a doe in closed season, which carried a one-hundred-dollar fine in those days. Ed had expected them to plead guilty and pay their fines. He couldn't help but wonder what kind of phony story they'd concocted, hoping that a judge would find them not guilty.

The hearing was held in front of Judge Samuel Richardson, the same judge with an extensive hunting background who had previously found Robert Lawless guilty of poaching several years earlier. And when the day finally arrived for Joe and Moe to plead their innocence in court, lo and behold, their father, Slim Skeever, strolled into the courtroom along with them.

Judge Richardson sat in stony silence behind his elevated mahogany desk as he reviewed the citations Ed Bond had filed weeks before. Ed and his deputy were seated in front of him on metal folding chairs, fifteen feet away and to his left. The Skeevers sat across from the wardens to the right of the judge.

When the judge lifted his eyes, he said, "I have two citations here, one for Joe Skeever and one for Moe Skeever. Are they in this courtroom?"

Both men raised their hands in acknowledgment.

Judge Richardson looked directly at Slim Skeever, his eyes like wounding arrows.

"And who are you?" he asked.

"I'm their father," Slim said. "Here to act as their attorney and represent them against the false charges that—"

Crack! The judge's gavel stuck the surface of his desk, cutting him off. "Stop right now," he warned, his voice was acid.

Slim sprang straight up from his seat. "But—"

Crack! came the gavel again. "One more word and I'll find you in contempt," the judge roared. "Now, sit down before I have these two wardens escort you directly to jail."

Slim plopped into his seat and scowled, his face a mask of disapproval.

"You're not an attorney, Mr. Skeever," the judge cautioned. "You won't be representing anyone. Stay if you wish but not another word out of you. Do you understand?"

Slim looked at the floor and nodded obediently.

Ed Bond was called first to testify. He gave precise details about the anonymous tip he'd received and how he and his deputy had come upon the Skeever brothers. He went on to testify about the blood on Joe Skeever's hands, the rifle he took from his truck, and the illegal doe that his brother had admitted killing. His deputy testified as well, backing up everything Ed had stated under oath.

When Ed and his deputy were finished, Joe and Moe Skeever were sworn in and had an opportunity to state their defense. Both men testified that they found the deer lying dead in the field. Mistaking it for roadkill, they wanted to keep it and were about to drive home to call the Game Commission for a permit when the game wardens swooped in on them.

When both men finished testifying, the judge leaned forward in his chair and eyed them critically.

"Roadkill, huh?" the judge questioned.

Both men nodded their heads yes.

The judge said, "One of the photos that Warden Bond submitted for evidence shows a gaping exit hole in the deer's chest. Did either of you happen to notice that?"

Both men shook their heads no.

"*Humph!*" the judge snorted. Then: "The wardens also testified that the deer's heart had been pulverized from the bullet as it exited its chest. Guess you never noticed that either when you removed the entrails."

Another no.

"And I heard testimony from Warden Bond that the rifle found in your truck had been recently fired."

"Target practice," Joe Skeever blurted. "We didn't shoot nothing."

"But what really astounds me," the judge continued as if he hadn't heard Skeever's remark, "is that neither of you said anything about a roadkilled deer when you were apprehended that night. In fact, I heard testimony from the wardens that Moe Skeever admitted to killing the deer."

Another blurt, this time from Moe: "But, we was—"

"*Silence!*" the judge boomed. "It's my turn to talk."

The brothers winced in unison.

"First and foremost, the game wardens need not prove you killed anything. You are both charged with *possession* of an unlawfully killed deer, not killing the animal, although I am convinced that that is precisely what you did. Secondly, I find your testimony to be completely unbelievable."

With that, the judge brought his gavel down one final time. "Guilty as charged," he said firmly. "The game wardens are excused, but the Skeever brothers will stay right here until they make arrangements to pay their fines."

However, Ed Bond's interactions with the Skeever family followed the traditional Rule of Three, with the final confrontation taking place several years later during the spring season. Appropriate considering that spring is commonly associated with rebirth and renewal.

As with many incidents involving poaching activity, the information had come to Ed through a phone call from an eyewitness. A young man named Cody was working at a service station in Newtown when he saw five does standing in an adjacent field along Route 413. He pointed out the deer to a coworker, who walked to the back of the shop and returned with a pair of binoculars for him. Although the deer were a good distance away, they could be easily observed with the field glasses.

While watching them, Cody heard a distant gunshot and saw one of the deer stagger and then drop. The deer kicked a few times and soon lay still. The young man was shocked and horrified by what he'd just seen. Deer season had ended months ago and he immediately called the Game Commission to report it.

Ed Bond was out of state at the time, so the dispatcher radioed a deputy who was checking trout fishermen with the local fish warden. The deputy quickly withdrew from the waterway and drove directly to the field where the deer had been shot, hoping to catch the poachers before they got away.

When he arrived, he saw the deer lying dead in the field but nobody was around. The nearest homes were on the opposite side of the highway, a considerable distance away. Too far, in his opinion, to bother knocking on doors to ask if anyone had seen or heard anything. And since the dispatcher had reported that the informant hadn't observed a vehicle or any sign of the shooter, the deputy considered the case closed and transported the carcass to the local rendering plant several miles away for disposal.

An entire week passed before the deputy reported the incident to Ed Bond. And although the deer was long gone and the trail cold, Ed wanted to see if he could still solve the case. His first step was to interview the young man who had reported the incident.

When Ed arrived at the service station, Cody was finishing up with an oil change on a customer's vehicle. Ed asked if he could break away for a moment to show him where the deer had been shot. After finding someone to cover for him, Cody walked out to the field with Ed, where they discovered a patch of dried blood in the grass where the deer had been killed. Ed asked the young man if he was certain that he hadn't seen a car stopped on the road or someone on foot with a gun, and he confirmed that he had not. However, he did mention the gunshot had been suppressed and suspected that it came from some distance away.

Ed focused on a cluster of eight houses across the road at the far end of the field. They were approximately three hundred yards away, their backyards facing him. If no vehicles were present when the deer was shot and nobody had been lurking around on foot, the bullet may have come from one of the eight houses.

Something was vaguely familiar about one of them, too, but Ed couldn't put his finger on it. He returned to his patrol car and grabbed his binoculars from the passenger seat. Raising the field glasses to his face, he focused on the eight homes. Seven boasted manicured lawns and upgraded exteriors, but the house in the middle stood out from the others with its unkempt lawn choked with gnarled weeds, shabby roof, and faded yellow siding.

Then it dawned on him and he realized who had killed the deer.

Slim Skeever lived there.

Ed had visited the house once before, years ago, after his first encounter with Slim when he had hidden the rifle in his pant leg. Ed suspected he would have another run-in with the man and had purposefully driven by his house so he would know where to find him quickly. He had only seen the place once and only from the front while cruising by in his patrol car that day, but he remembered its dull yellow siding, the unkempt lawn, and that it was located on a cul-de-sac in the center of seven other homes near Route 413.

Ed drove directly to the circle of homes, stopping two doors south of Skeever's house to knock. An elderly man with thinning white hair and thick horn-rimmed glasses answered. Ed told him about the deer shot earlier in the week along Route 413 and that he suspected the poacher lived close by.

"I heard a rifle shot last week," the man replied. "It came from one of the homes here, I can tell you that. Not the first time either."

"Can you tell me who it was?"

He shook his head no. "Sorry, but I don't want any trouble with my neighbors. You'll have to figure that out on your own." Then, he slowly stepped back and closed the door.

Ed went to the house next to Slim Skeever's and asked the same question. They claimed to know nothing about it.

He skipped Skeever's house and went two houses north. The occupants said they knew about a deer that had been killed near Route 413 but didn't know who was responsible.

Ed felt sure everyone knew Slim Skeever killed the deer but were too scared to say. Skeever was known to have a bad temper and had a history of violence. He detested law enforcement officers—game wardens in particular.

Realizing it was useless to keep knocking on doors, hoping for a witness willing to talk, the time had come for a showdown with the man.

Slim Skeever answered the knock on his door wearing a sleeveless undershirt and grungy old blue jeans. He looked surprised when he saw Ed but quickly regained himself. "You lost or something, game warden?" he grunted.

"I'm here about the deer," Ed said.

The reply was as expected. "What deer?"

"You know exactly what deer," Ed said evenly. "The one you shot last Saturday on Route 413."

Skeever said nothing. He just stood in the doorway, defiant and grinning like a fool. With no physical evidence or witnesses to support him, Ed knew the odds of cracking the case were stacked against him. He also realized that Skeever wouldn't admit to anything. But at the very least, he thought Skeever would be aware that he was onto him, and perhaps that would keep him from shooting across the road, endangering passing motorists.

But Slim had made the fatal mistake of leaving the front door open, and his rotund wife—the physical opposite of her rangy husband—had overheard the warden's accusation.

"I told you not to shoot that deer in the first place!" she bellowed from behind him.

Slim ducked his head into his shoulders and cringed at her bitter voice.

Then he looked at Ed and shook his head in weary resignation. "How much is this going to cost me?"

Ed told him two hundred dollars.

His wife put her hands on her ample hips, her face twisting into an ugly scowl. "And don't you dare ask me to lend you one single penny, mister!"

Apparently, the risk of facing his wife's wrath was more than Slim could bear, for he quickly made arrangements with

Ed to pay his fine, hoping to reconcile with her and put the incident behind him.

In the end, Slim's wife turned out to be the only evidence Ed had against him, and although a wife is not required to testify against her husband in a court of law, as mad as she sounded, she may have done just that.

"Who killed Cock Robin?"
"I," said the sparrow,
"With my bow and arrow,
I killed Cock Robin."
      ~Anonymous Nursery Rhyme

A SHOT IN THE DARK

RETURNING HOME after a long shift at the hospital, Dr. Gray wanted nothing more than to jump into bed and sleep until noon. It was one o'clock in the morning and he was exhausted.

    He was the doctor on call for the emergency room at the hospital when an ambulance brought in a motorcycle crash victim just as his shift was ending. The biker was stopped at a traffic light when a pickup truck hit his Harley-Davidson from behind. The motorcycle was totaled. The victim's injuries were life-threatening. Unconscious and bloody, his face was grossly distended twice its size and his eyes were swollen shut. Blood trickled from his nose and mouth and large patches of skin were missing on the left side of his body.

    Dr. Gray suspected internal injuries and had him wheeled into the operating room, where he performed emergency surgery for a punctured lung and multiple bone fractures.

The surgery had taken several hours and by the time it was over, Dr. Gray had put in a fourteen-hour shift and had visited dozens of patients, the accident victim being the worst by far.

He was almost home. Traffic had been non-existent since he'd left the hospital, for which he was thankful. It had been a thirty-minute drive and he'd nearly dozed off along the way. Shaken, he powered down his windows so the rush of cold air would keep him awake. He switched on his radio, the volume high. The Rolling Stones were singing *Jumpin' Jack Flash*, and the upbeat music influenced his mood. Suddenly he felt alive. It was magical!

He never expected to hit a deer while driving home, admiring his spacious two-story house under the moonlit sky.

Just before turning into his driveway, the doe appeared out of nowhere and Dr. Gray struck it with his Toyota Sequoia SUV. The deer went down hard, then quickly sprang up and dashed into a patch of trees at the edge of his yard.

As the doctor continued driving up his driveway, his headlights startled a small herd of deer in his neighbor's yard. One deer, a doe, did not run away with the others and he took that as an indication that it was the one he had hit moments before.

He assumed that the deer must have been severely injured, similar to the man who had been hurt in the motorcycle crash he had worked on hours earlier. After all, both were victims of the sudden impact of a vehicle. But unlike the man who survived the motorcycle accident, there was nothing Dr. Gray could do to stop the blood loss or heal broken bones for the injured deer.

Therefore, it had to be put down. He thought it was the only humane thing to do in this case.

The doe stood frozen in the flood of his neighbor's exterior property lights as Dr. Gray pulled his vehicle inside the garage and parked. He slid out of his car, quietly closed the door so as not to spook the injured animal, and walked to the front of his car to inspect the damage.

Ugh! It was definitely going to cost him.

To his right hung a bow from a hook on the garage wall. A collection of arrows was spread out on the workbench directly below. He took the bow from the wall and lifted an arrow from the bench. Padding over to the open garage door, he stepped outside and nocked his arrow securely into the bowstring. Keeping his eyes on the deer twenty yards away, he pulled back on the bowstring, took careful aim, and released.

He knew the deer had been hit when he heard a dull thump as the arrow struck flesh. But instead of dropping to the ground, mortally wounded as he had envisioned, the doe promptly ran off.

Dr. Gray watched in utter dismay as the deer vanished into the night. Hoping to find it lying dead nearby, he hurried back into his garage for a flashlight and went out to search for it. But it was late and he was exhausted. After a brief search, he trudged back home and went to bed. Tomorrow was another day, he thought. He would search for it again in the morning light.

He didn't find it then, either.

It was his first week on the job as a freshly graduated state game warden when Jesse Cunningham received a call from a woman who reported that she had found a dead deer with an arrow sticking out of it in the front yard of her suburban home. She had been unaware of the deer until her dog found the carcass under a pine tree at the edge of her property. Mortified that someone would be shooting and killing wildlife in a heavily residential area, she pleaded for Jesse to come out right away and catch whoever was responsible.

Jesse drove directly to the woman's house in his state-issued patrol car. He was in full uniform as he approached the front door, hoping the complainant could provide additional information that might lead him to the perpetrator.

He knocked, and a woman in her mid-thirties came to the door with a dishtowel in her hands.

"Thank you for coming so soon," she said. "I've kept my children inside all day so they wouldn't see the poor creature lying there. The crows pecked out its eyes. I'm afraid the sight of it might scar them for life."

Jesse asked if she'd seen any people or vehicles in the neighborhood that were new to her.

She had not.

Had she seen anyone hunting or carrying a bow recently?

Another no.

Did she have any idea who might have shot the deer?

She did not.

"Will you be able to take the deer away?" she asked, her face lined with concern.

Jesse told her he had a big game rack attached to the back of his vehicle and assured her he would remove the deer from her property after examining the carcass.

"Thank you, officer," she said. "My children want to go out and play in the yard and I'm running out of excuses."

With no tips from the woman that might lead him to the perpetrator, he walked back to the deer, a medium-sized doe, and performed a necropsy. The animal had been there for more than a day. It had been shot through the heart by an arrow equipped with a field tip instead of a broadhead. As a result, the deer had died of internal hemorrhaging without leaving a blood trail to follow.

After canvassing the immediate area, with no one having witnessed any suspicious vehicles or hunting activity, Jesse believed he had little chance of solving the case. The area was frequented by many deer, evident from the complaints he'd received in recent days about damage to ornamental plants and shrubbery. Perhaps someone saw the deer feeding on their shrubs and took a shot at it. The neighborhood was huge. It could have been anyone.

Nevertheless, the warden did notice some custom work on the arrow's build that made it unique, and he thought it might lead him to the perpetrator. He planned to visit several archery pro-shops in the area to see if any of them had designed the arrow when he caught an unexpected break in the case.

The next morning, a man called to report that he had recently tried to put down an injured deer with his bow but was unable to recover the carcass and needed help. Jesse asked for his address and was surprised to learn that he lived near the woman with the dead doe on her property. When he asked for his name, he told him it was Dr. Gray.

Jesse went to Dr. Gray's house and showed him the arrow he'd extracted from the dead doe on his neighbor's property. Dr. Gray admitted it was his and explained how he'd hit the deer with his car and decided to "do the humane thing" and put it out of its misery.

He went on to say that he'd tried bowhunting once and didn't care for it but enjoyed target shooting in his back yard and practiced regularly, which clarified why the arrow had a field point rather than a broadhead and how he was able to make such an accurate shot.

Jesse explained how the arrow's flight could have led to an injury for a neighbor or someone's pet had he missed. After all, it was a shot in the dark.

Dr. Gray thought about that possibility, admittedly for the first time, and started to feel remorse for taking a risk that could have injured someone, especially while working toward the health and safety of his patients throughout his career as a doctor.

Regardless of his feelings, Jesse explained that he would be filing a citation against him for killing the deer because nothing he did could be construed as a good idea, no matter his intentions.

He shot at a deer during a closed hunting season, in the dark, without a hunting license, and in the middle of a residential neighborhood.

Jesse wrapped up his interview with Dr. Gray by explaining that only certain law enforcement officers and veterinarians are allowed to euthanize wildlife, as they have the training it takes to do it safely and ethically.

He thought it unfortunate that the physician hadn't remembered one of the primary tenets of his profession.

Doctors are to follow the Hippocratic Oath, which says, "First, do no harm."

He did the opposite, taking a bad situation and making it worse, and was lucky nobody got hurt.

When Daniel Boone goes by at night
The phantom deer arise
And all lost, wild America
Is burning in their eyes.
 ~Stephen Vincent Benét

WITH DEER

"THE LIFE OF A GAME WARDEN was much slower back in the sixties," recalled Ed Bond during a recent phone call with him.

We speak regularly, and I marvel at how well he remembers his days afield, even while in his nineties.

"Much of the time, you found yourself sitting behind a steering wheel or a typewriter," he said. "Now, it's a computer. I hear they even have them in their patrol cars."

"Yes, they do," I said. "Times have changed."

"They certainly have. In 1960, when I first came on, you used your own automobile. The Game Commission paid for the gasoline. You bought a desk and a typewriter and were on duty twenty-four hours a day. We operated out of our homes and were at the mercy of anyone who paid their phone bill last month. Many times, I was called out in the middle of the night to dispatch a deer that had been hit by a car and was still alive. A pathetic situation."

He paused for a moment, then said, "Before I retired after thirty-five years of service, I was picking up between eight and ten roadkilled deer every day. One day, I picked up twenty."

"Twenty in one day!" I gasped. "That's more than most game wardens pick up in a month. Six months for some."

"There was no place to put them, either," he continued. "So I had to drive all the way up to the rendering plant in Montgomery County to dispose of the carcasses. A forty-mile round trip."

"There must have been days when all you did was pick up dead deer," I said.

"Too many of them," he replied. "Bucks County was crawling with deer back then. Many landowners posted 'no hunting' signs, and with all the highways and traffic everywhere, the deer didn't stand a chance."

I nodded in agreement, even though he couldn't see me.

"I had some unusual experiences while dealing with deer that were hit by a car but not killed," he said. "I remember one time when a lady hit a doe in Buckingham Township. She was there when I arrived and was in tears over what she had done. The deer was far from saving, so I shot it and loaded it onto my deer rack.

"Thinking she might somehow be at fault for hitting the deer, the poor woman asked, 'Now, what's going to happen to me?' So I looked at her and said, 'Well, I'm certainly not going to shoot you, too.' We both had a good laugh and she went happily on her way.

"Another experience I had was back in the seventies when I received a call about a deer that had been hit in Solebury Township.

"When I arrived on the scene, the car was still there with a man sitting behind the wheel. I asked him about the deer and he simply pointed across the road but said nothing. I looked and saw a blanket with a rather large lump under it, so I walked over and pulled the blanket back, and to my horror and surprise, I discovered a woman with her arms wrapped tightly around a very dead doe. She was crying uncontrollably."

"Good grief!" I breathed.

"That's what I thought, too," Ed said. "Anyway, with some difficulty, I was able to loosen her grip while attempting to console her at the same time. She was having none of it and once again resumed her hold on the deer.

"Finally, her husband came over, and between the two of us, we got her on her feet and into their car. I really felt sorry for her. She probably thought she had killed the only deer in Bucks County…little did she know."

Growing up in Bucks County, I understood the mindset of some people living in this heavily populated area just outside Philadelphia. We referred to them as bunny-huggers, tree-huggers, and animal rights whackos. Regardless of what they were called, they shared the same frame of mind.

"For years, it was unlawful to possess a roadkilled deer in Pennsylvania," Ed recalled. "In the late seventies, the Game Commission initiated a permit system where if someone killed a deer with their vehicle, they could be issued a permit to possess the animal.

"But there were always some folks who thought they were above the law, especially state game laws. We called them poachers, game hogs, hoofties, or just plain outlaws. One person I'll never forget was an arrogant, township police officer whose power went to his head. Want to hear about it?"

"Of course!" I said, leaning closer to the phone.

"It went like this…"

One evening in October back in the sixties, Deputy Noah Miller was called out to pick up a roadkilled deer. In those days, deer killed on highways were not allowed to be possessed by motorists at any time or under any circumstances.

When Noah pulled his pickup truck to the side of the road and parked next to the deer, Chief Al Onerous came cruising down the highway in his marked patrol car and stopped behind him with the red bubble light on his roof activated.

Onerous was the chief of a one-cop police force. Meaning he was it. Even so, he had an imperious attitude toward almost everyone he met, especially if they wore a badge, and most notably if they happened to be deputy game wardens, whom he considered to be as useless as lips on a chicken.

Noah knew all about the chief and chose to ignore him. As he dragged the dead deer toward his truck, he heard the chief's car door creak open and slam shut behind him.

"Hey! I want that deer," the Chief hollered.

Noah kept his back turned as he dropped the tailgate and loaded the deer into his truck.

"Hey, you!" the chief cried. "You deaf or what? I said I want that deer!"

Noah shoved the carcass deep into the bed and slammed the tailgate shut. Then he turned to face Onerous.

The chief was in full uniform, sporting navy blue pants, a powder blue shirt complete with a brass badge, no tie, polished black shoes, and a black leather holster equipped with a .38 Special Smith & Wesson revolver.

In his mid-forties, his premature gray hair was cut Marine Corps short, his face set in a perpetual scowl, eyes dark and brooding. Onerous had been a bully all his life; his fondest memories were of his high school years when he would walk the halls challenging anyone who dared to hold his gaze. One explosive punch to the gut would solve that problem fast.

He had many fights and never lost.

And he loved being a cop.

Unlike the chief, Deputy Noah Miller was not wearing a uniform and was unarmed at the time. He'd been called about the deer just before dinner and lived close by, so he decided to quickly retrieve the carcass and return to his house for a meal with his family.

"I can't give you the deer," he told the chief.

Onerous folded his arms across his heavy chest and glared at the deputy. "Sure, you can," he snorted. "Drop your tailgate and I'll take it off your hands."

"Can't do it," Noah repeated. "The law doesn't allow for it and you would be in violation for possessing a deer in closed season if I let you take it."

Onerous turned his head and spat a thin stream of brown tobacco juice inches from Noah's feet. "That's the stupidest law I ever heard of. It's a dead deer! Who cares what happens to it?"

Noah shrugged. "I don't make the laws; I just enforce them...same as you're supposed to do."

Chief Onerous stiffened, his face turning scarlet. "Who do you think you're talking to?" he hissed. "This is *my* township, deputy. *I'm* the law around here. You can bet the next time a deer gets hit by a car, the Game Commission won't hear anything about it."

Noah thought it best not to say anything; the chief had a short fuse. Not wanting to antagonize him further, he turned and began walking toward the cab of his truck.

"Better make sure I never catch you driving over the speed limit," the chief warned from behind. "Not even one mile per hour too fast.

"You hear me, deputy? Not even *one mile per hour!*"

Later that day, Chief Onerous sat in front of his TV watching the Philadelphia Eagles play against the New York Giants. He loved football but his earlier encounter with the deputy hung in the room like a bad dream and took away from the game.

Onerous poured himself another half-glass of Jack Daniels and knocked it back in a single gulp. The whiskey warmed his throat and chest before radiating into his arms, legs, and head. It was his only friend, the whiskey, and it always made him feel more at ease, especially after that third glass. But this had been his fifth pour and it wasn't helping.

A nice venison steak would have made the game so much more enjoyable. But for a bit of respect from that lowly deputy, he'd be munching on one right now. He was the law here. It was *his* township. Bestowed upon him by the Board of

Supervisors, whom he likened to *The Three Stooges*—only there were five of them, which made them even more crackbrained.

Onerous poured himself another drink, raised the glass and stared into the golden liquid. There was only one way to set things right—to make the *world* right as far as he was concerned: the deputy would have to answer for his insubordination. Onerous knew where he lived. Knew where he worked, too. And life would soon become more challenging for Deputy Noah Miller.

Yes, the deputy would have to pay...of that he was certain.

Chief Onerous sat alone in his patrol car as he minded the speed trap he'd set along Route 413 the night before. It was the perfect place to nab motorists exceeding the speed limit of fifty-five miles per hour at this particular stretch of the road. Hemmed on both sides by unharvested cornfields, it was a wide-open straightaway with plenty of room to pass for anyone in a hurry.

Onerous had marked the blacktop with narrow, white-painted lines one hundred yards apart. In those days, there were no handheld radar guns, so police officers often used a chart that converted miles per hour into yards per second to enforce the speed limit. The chart specified that vehicles traveling fifty-five miles per hour would take four seconds to travel one hundred yards. Thus, the two white lines.

Onerous had backed his patrol car into a section of standing corn directly in front of the painted lines so he wouldn't be spotted by passing motorists. He had a stopwatch in his right hand and the speed chart lying on his lap as he gazed out the windshield, waiting for Deputy Noah Miller to come by. As for the corn flattened by his patrol car, it would be a small price for the farmer to pay to support law and order in his township.

The flat tire Noah had discovered earlier that morning had held him up and he was running late for work as he drove along Route 413 toward the steel plant. Someone had slashed the rubber sidewall on one of his back tires. The tire was ruined and would be expensive to replace. It could have been worse, he thought, and in a way, he felt lucky. They could have slashed all four, which would have cost him a day's wages.

Deputy Miller worried that whoever was responsible might return to do more damage to his truck. He thought about leaving his German shepherd tied out at night for a few weeks as he cruised toward the mill. He had a wife, Sarah, and two girls, Esther and Joanna, at home He barely made enough money to get by. The last thing he needed was more bills.

Deputy game wardens were volunteers and received no pay. They used their own vehicles and paid for their gas out of pocket. They also bought their own firearms and leather gear. If they were lucky enough to be offered a uniform to wear, that would cost them as well. They were—and still are—dedicated individuals who wanted nothing more than to protect our natural resources and preserve our hunting heritage for generations to come. And Deputy Noah Miller was one of the best.

Chief Onerous knew that Deputy Miller would be running late as he shot out his wrist and glanced at his Timex watch. Should be any minute now, he thought. The chief had done his homework. He knew where Noah lived and where he worked. He knew when he left in the morning and how long it took him to get to the steel mill. And, most importantly, he knew how long it would take to change that flat tire. Yessiree Bob. It would soon be time to pay the piper.

When Deputy Miller drove over the chief's painted white lines in his green Ford pickup, it took exactly four seconds. Chief Onerous shook his head and chuckled sarcastically to himself. *A genuine Dudley Do-Right,* he thought. *The guy is late for work and he still obeys the speed limit.*
Loser!

Noah Miller squinted into the rearview mirror when he heard the shrill *whoop-whoop-whoop* from behind. Chief Onerous was so close he could see his grim face. Stetson hat clamped tight to his head, black aviator sunglasses shielding his eyes, fat lips pressed into a sneer of contempt.

Noah glanced at the speedometer; the needle pointed straight at fifty-five. Why was he being pulled over? He wasn't speeding. Thinking a taillight might be out, he switched on his turn signal, wheeled to the right shoulder of the road and stopped.

Noah rolled down his window and stared into his sideview mirror as Chief Onerous exited his patrol car and strolled toward him in full uniform. He seemed deliberately slow, almost painfully slow, as he approached. Noah glanced at his wristwatch and felt a stab in his stomach. He was already thirty minutes late for work and pictured his boss standing by the time clock with his hands on his hips, waiting for him to punch in. Noah was the shop boss and head welder responsible for fabricating truck mufflers. He played an integral role in the assembly line. Without him, the production process would come to a standstill.

License and registration," the chief grunted.

"Why are you stopping me?" Noah asked as he dug into his back pocket and produced a worn leather wallet.

The chief dropped his chin and spat a stream of brown juice between his boots. Then he locked eyes with Noah and grinned, his teeth stained from years of chewing tobacco. "You know how fast you were going?"

"I wasn't speeding," Noah said as he handed his driver's license to the cop.

"Speed limit is fifty-five. I clocked you at seventy. What's the hurry, got another roadkill to pick up before somebody else gets it?"

"So that's what this is about," Noah shot back angrily. "You're still mad about the deer. You know I wasn't speeding."

"Go tell it to the judge," said Onerous. "We'll see who he believes—you or me."

A Harley-Davidson motorcycle blew by, narrowly missing the chief as he stood on the edge of the blacktop. Loud and obnoxious, it thundered down the highway at an easy eighty miles per hour. The rider wore a leather jacket with a *Warlocks MC* logo on the back.

Noah shook his head as he watched the biker disappear around a bend. "That's who you should be after: crazies like that guy on the motorcycle."

"What motorcycle?" Onerous asked, deadpan. Then he turned and started walking back to his patrol car with Noah's license in hand. "Stay right there," he called over his shoulder. "Gonna write you a ticket. Might take me a while. Feeling a little lazy this morning."

Later that week, Noah's daughters were seated on the bus on their way to school when it stopped suddenly. Both girls leaned forward and peered out the long bank of windows on their left. They saw a police car with its emergency lights flashing, parked behind a vehicle with noticeable damage to its front end. A police officer stood by the damaged vehicle and waved the bus on. As they passed, the girls spotted a dead eight-point buck on the side of the road.

Later that evening, as the family gathered for dinner, the girls told their father about the deer, unaware of his previous encounters with the chief.

Since there was only one patrolman in the entire township, Noah knew the police officer had to be Chief Onerous. And because he hadn't been contacted to pick up the deer, he called Ed Bond to see if he knew anything about it. Ed informed Noah that there was no report of any deer being killed along the highway near the school and asked him to speak with Chief Onerous about it.

Noah couldn't wait to see him again.

Deputy Noah Miller stopped by the township building the following day after finishing his shift at the mill. The chief's patrol car was parked outside, so he knew he was there. He stepped through the front door of the brick building and walked down a long block corridor toward the chief's office. Noah could hear Onerous arguing with someone on the phone as he approached, his voice loud and angry as it bounced off the walls in the hallway. When he reached his office and saw the door wide open, he let himself in without knocking.

The chief's conversation suddenly trailed off, his heavy jaw slackening as the deputy appeared. He quickly caught himself and hung up, bringing his quarrel to an abrupt end.

Chief Onerous sat at his desk, glowering at Noah. "If you're here to ask me to toss your speeding ticket, you can turn around and walk right back out that door."

"I'm here about the deer," Noah replied.

The chief's stern glare softened for a moment, barely perceptible but Noah caught it. "What are you talking about?"

"A buck was hit near the middle school yesterday. You were seen standing on the road by the damaged car and the deer."

Onerous hesitated, then: "Oh, that deer," he said, dismissing the incident with a wave of his hand. "It jumped up and ran off right after I got there. It's long gone by now."

Noah suspected he was lying but played it cool. "Happens sometimes," he said. "All I need is the police report and I'll be on my way."

"You don't need that," the chief said. "I already told you the deer ran off."

"Ed Bond absolutely wants the report," Noah said. "You can give it to me now, or he'll get it from your supervisor later. It's up to you."

Onerous stared at the deputy for a long moment. Then he reached down and yanked open a desk drawer and rifled through a row of manila folders until he found what he was looking for. Pulling a document from one of the folders, he swiveled in his chair toward the Xerox machine on the table beside him and inserted it into its mouth. Onerous pushed a button on its side and the machine hummed for a moment before spitting out a copy of the police report.

The chief snatched the report from the machine and propelled it across his desk with a flip of his wrist. "Satisfied, deputy?" he asked. His tone was sharp.

Noah took the document from his desk and looked at him. "Ask me again in an hour," he said.

Deputy Miller had just pulled into his driveway after dropping off the police report with Ed Bond when his neighbor, Jeff Lynch, walked by with his Labrador retriever, Sally and waved hello.

Noah waved back and began walking toward the front door when Jeff called out to him. "Everything okay with your truck?"

Noah froze, then turned to face him. "What do you mean?"

Jeff walked up the driveway until he was close enough to speak in low tones.

"Don't mean to be nosy," he said, "but the other day, Sally was barking by the door at two in the morning. She only does that if she has to go real bad, so I got dressed and took her out to do her business when I saw Chief Onerous crouched by the back of your truck. He was only there for a few seconds before he walked back to his car and drove off. You being a game warden and all, I wondered if he was checking for a bomb or something."

Noah was stunned but managed to keep a straight face with the realization that Chief Onerous must have been the one who had slashed his tire a few days ago.

Noah shrugged coolly. "Who knows? Maybe he clipped a raccoon or a possum and it ran under my truck. Probably just checking to see if it was okay."

"So no bombs or anything, huh?"

"Nope. No bombs. It looks like I'm going to live another day."

"Good to hear. I watch a lot of cop shows on TV. Some of those car bombs are powerful enough to take out my house right along with your truck."

Ed Bond was in his office sorting through a stack of paperwork when Noah Miller had stopped by earlier with the police report. The report stated that a 1957 Chevrolet Impala had struck a deer near the middle school and sustained moderate damage to its front end. It listed the vehicle's operator as Martin Lemsky, who lived in Pittstown, New Jersey.

Chief Onerous had failed to include the driver's telephone number in the report. Ed couldn't help but wonder if he'd done it intentionally. To make matters worse, Martin Lemsky lived out of state, and a hundred-mile round trip based on the chance that Lemsky would be home when Ed arrived unannounced was a long shot at best.

Fortunately, after jumping through a few hoops, Ed connected with a telephone operator who serviced the Pittstown area. He asked if she had a phone number for Martin Lemsky and was told it was unlisted. Ed then asked if any other listings in Pittston had the same last name. There was only one, and she gave him the phone number.

Ed dialed the number with his fingers crossed. When a male voice answered, Ed identified himself as a Pennsylvania state game warden and asked if he happened to be related to Martin Lemsky.

"Yes, I am," the man answered. "He's my brother. What's this all about?"

"Did your brother ever say anything about a deer he hit in Bucks County, Pennsylvania?"

"He didn't have to; I was with him when he hit it. A nice eight-pointer."

Ed said, "Well, then maybe you can clear something up for me. I spoke to a witness who told me that the deer got up and ran off after it was hit. Is that true?"

"I don't know what deer they were talking about," said the man. "This one was dead as a doornail."

"Can you tell me what happened to it?"

"It was strapped to the hood of a police car the last time I saw it. Why don't you ask *them* about it?"

"I intend to," Ed said. "Thanks for your help."

"Hey, I have a quick question before you go."

"Sure thing," Ed replied.

"Does your agency cover the damages when someone hits one of your deer?"

The next day, Ed Bond went to the township building to see Chief Onerous about the deer. On his way into the building, he bumped into a tall, well-dressed man in a tie and sports coat. Ed was in his uniform, including his Stetson hat.

"Game warden!" the man said in surprise. "Can I help you?"

"I'm here to see Chief Onerous."

He pointed down the cinderblock hallway. "Last door on the right." The man paused, then extended his hand. "I'm Jed Stevens, President of the Board of Supervisors for the township. What's this about, if you don't mind me asking?"

Ed met his gaze. "I have a few questions about a deer hit by a car a few days ago."

Stevens' eyes narrowed, his voice dropping to a curious murmur. "Is there anything I should know about?"

"That would depend on how cooperative the chief is when I talk to him."

Stevens reached into the breast pocket of his sports coat, pulled out a business card and handed it to Ed. "Give me a call if you need anything, warden. We've had more than a few complaints about the chief."

"I'll do that," Ed said.

Stevens nodded. "Keep me in the know, okay?"

Chief Onerous stopped typing and looked up when Ed Bond entered his office. "Why aren't you out in the woods harassing honest hunters?" he said with a mocking edge to his voice.

"Because I'm here to see you."

"Is this about that stupid deer again?" the chief snorted. He slid his chair back and stood by his desk. "I told your deputy yesterday that the deer got up and ran off. Now, why don't you turn around and go back to wherever you came from?"

"Because that's not what happened."

Chief Onerous raised an eyebrow. "Oh, really. Says who?"

"I have two witnesses that saw you strap the deer to the hood of your car and drive off with it," Ed told him.

Ed watched the blood drain from the chief's face. "You, what…?"

"The Lemsky brothers from Pittstown, New Jersey. Ring a bell? I got the information from your police report and called them yesterday."

Onerous paused, his eyes searching the room for an answer. Realizing he was caught, he shrugged offhandedly. "So okay. I took it. I mean, why let good venison go to waste?"

"It's a fifty-dollar fine," Ed said. "You can take a court hearing or pay on a field acknowledgment of guilt. It's your choice."

The chief folded his heavy arms and fixed Ed with a hard glare. "You do this to me and I'm gonna get even. Just like I did with your deputy, you can count on it."

Ed's brow furrowed. "What are you talking about?"

"Speeding." Onerous said. "Ask him about it."

Caught off guard, Ed quickly shook the news out of his head. "Citation or field receipt?" he pressed. "Your choice."

Ed knew the chief would never take a hearing and risk having his face plastered on the front page of the local newspaper. And they both knew there was little chance he would win in front of the justice of the peace, an avid hunter who always went by the book. The fact that the chief had absconded with a trophy eight-point buck would have riled the judge to no end, even if it was only a roadkill.

Onerous looked at Ed and flashed a crooked smile. "You win," he said, his voice low. "This time, anyway."

The chief pulled a wallet from his back pocket, took a fifty-dollar bill from inside and laid it on his desk. Got the paperwork? I'll pay you right now."

"What did you do with the deer?" Ed asked.

"Gave it away."

"Away where?"

Onerous shrugged. "Don't remember."

Ed said, "I ran into Jed Stevens on my way into the building. He gave me his business card. Said to call him if I needed anything."

Onerous paused, then looked away and shook his head in resignation. "Man, you guys never quit, do you?"

"No, we don't. Now, where is the deer?"

"I took it to the butcher shop down the road," he said. "They still have it."

Ed reached into his jacket pocket and pulled out a blank field acknowledgment of guilt and a ballpoint pen.

He began to write.

Luigi's butcher shop was a familiar place for most folks, especially hunters. And with archery deer season open, Ed expected they'd be working on several fresh carcasses. Hunting pressure was heavy in those days with the overabundance of deer in the county.

When Ed arrived, three cars were in the parking lot. He recognized the vehicles; they belonged to the men who worked there. He felt relieved, as he didn't want to confront the owner with customers nearby.

Ed nosed his car up to the red brick building and parked. An orange neon sign blazed in the front window that said, THE BUTCHER SHOP. He circled to the back of the building, where a separate structure the size of a three-car garage had been added years ago to handle his thriving deer processing business.

When Ed entered the shop, all eyes turned to him. The atmosphere inside was cool and slightly chilly, helping to preserve the deer meat. The interior walls were lined with white tiles for easy cleaning, and the air was thick with the pungent scent of raw deer meat.

All three men wore aprons. Two had white ones, while the third man wore a brown leather apron like the traditional butchers of old. They had all been working on deer carcasses, their aprons stained with blood and gore as they stood by stainless steel counters used to break down whole deer into specific cuts. Behind them stood a row of industrial-grade meat slicers, grinders, and bandsaws for processing venison.

"I'm here to pick up the deer that Chief Onerous dropped off," Ed announced.

The man in the brown apron put down his knife and stepped toward him.

"I am Luigi," he said with a thick Italian accent. "I own this place. I don't know nothing about this deer you talk about. We are very busy. Please go and come back later."

Ed took a step toward him. "I think you know exactly what I'm talking about. The chief brought in an eight-point buck earlier this week."

"It's not here," Luigi insisted. "Now, please go. We have much work to do."

Having had enough of Luigi for the time being, Ed informed him that he had just arrested their chief of police for possessing the deer unlawfully, and if he didn't turn it over to him, he would arrest all three of them as well.

Luigi suddenly had a change of heart. "No need for arrests," he said. "I get it for you. Then you leave."

Luigi turned and walked into a room at the back. He emerged moments later carrying a cardboard box filled with packages wrapped in brown butcher paper. Luigi placed the box on a wooden block table by the door and looked at Ed. "You pay me now," he said.

Ed said. "I'm not paying for it; I'm confiscating it."

Word travels fast in some places, especially in rural areas like Bucks County in the 60s. Luigi couldn't get over the fact that he wasn't getting paid for the deer he had butchered. The chief wouldn't return his calls and refused to discuss the matter with him. That turned out to be a mistake because, in turn, Luigi called the township supervisors and demanded payment for the deer, which led to an investigation into the chiefs' behavior.

When the supervisors discovered that the deer had been unlawfully possessed and subsequently seized by a state game warden, it was the last straw for Chief Onerous. The township issued him two weeks' notice and placed an advertisement in the *Philadelphia Inquirer* for his position on the same day.

The chief's dismissal meant that the speeding ticket he'd fabricated against Noah Miller would go nowhere. Noah had requested a court hearing, and after learning about the chief's removal, the judge dismissed the charge and informed Noah that he did not have to appear in court.

Local jobs were scarce in those days, and the chief had little choice but to apply for a position at the steel mill. It was nearby, and he had worked there for several years before becoming a police officer.

On his first day at the plant, he was assigned to operate a seam welder on an assembly line for the production of truck mufflers.

His supervisor was Noah Miller.

Yesterday is not ours to recover, but tomorrow is ours to win or to lose. I am resolved that we shall win the tomorrows before us.
    ~Lyndon B. Johnson

WIN SOME, LOSE SOME

D RIVING ALONG STUMP ROAD in Bucks County back in 1965, Game Warden Ed Bond spotted a cardboard box in a snowy field several yards from the road. The snow was fresh, indicating it had been dumped earlier that day. He saw footprints leading from the road to the box and back again. A littering violation to be sure, but Ed suspected there might be more, so he stopped his patrol car and walked over for a closer look. When he opened the box, he discovered the head and hide of a recently killed doe.

It was mid-January. Deer season was closed.

A label on the box with a tracking number confirmed that UPS had shipped it, but the recipient's name and address had been torn off. Confident that the shipping company could trace the number, Ed took the box to the UPS trucking terminal twenty miles away in Chalfont.

Ed was in his Game Commission uniform when he stepped inside the building and approached the front desk. An attractive young woman typing reports looked up at him and smiled. "How can I help you, officer?"

Ed had copied the tracking number from the box onto a slip of paper. He showed it to her and asked if she could tell him where the box had been delivered.

"I'm so sorry," she said, "but the driver for that area is still making deliveries. If you come back at three o'clock, he should be here. I'll make sure he waits for you, too."

Ed glanced at his watch. It was just past noon. "I'll do that," he said. "Thanks for your help."

She observed his uniform briefly. "Park ranger, right?"

"State Game Commission," Ed corrected.

Her pretty blue eyes grew wide with wonder. "Oh, that must be the best job *ever!* What kind of games do you play…?"

With several hours to kill waiting for the UPS driver to return, Ed was patrolling the northern end of his district when he spotted a distant hunter making his way through a weedy snowfield. The hunter wore a safety orange ball cap and vest with brown canvas pants and a matching coat. A hunting license was pinned to his back.

With small game season open for squirrels, rabbits, and grouse, Ed assumed he was hunting rabbits. He pulled to the side of the road as the man plodded through the snow, unaware that he was being observed.

To Ed's surprise, a hen ringneck pheasant exploded from the field and the hunter blasted the bird with his shotgun at point-blank range. The pheasant spun in the air once and tumbled to the ground in a heap of feathers.

Ed continued to watch as the hunter retrieved the bird and stuffed it into a game pouch in the back of his coat. Pheasant season had closed long ago.

In those days, game wardens did not have loudspeakers, sirens, or even red lights on their cars. To make matters worse, Ed was driving a Ford sedan, incapable of navigating the heavy snow that separated him from the hunter, a good hundred yards away.

Ed honked his horn to get the man's attention before clamping on his Stetson hat and climbing out of his car.

"State game warden!" he called, waving him over. "Come out of the field."

The hunter waved back and began to trudge through the six-inch-deep snow toward Ed with his shotgun held abreast.

When he was fifteen feet away, Ed signaled for him to stop and unload his pump shotgun.

"Is there a problem, officer?" he asked as he cycled the action, ejecting three shells into his hand.

"What's your name?" Ed asked.

"Forrest Frostbow," he said, stuffing the live rounds into a coat pocket.

Ed stepped toward him. "Turn around. I want to check your game bag."

Frostbow did as he was told and Ed reached inside, retrieving the pheasant he'd shot.

"Pheasant season is closed," Ed told him.

Frostbow spun around, his face a mixture of confusion and surprise. "Pheasant…? I thought it was a grouse!"

"You'd be hard-pressed to find a ruffed grouse in this part of the state," Ed said. "Besides, they're a woodland bird, not an agricultural bird. This is a female ring-necked pheasant. They're protected by the Game Commission and the fine is twenty-five dollars."

Frostbow looked at the bird and then back at Ed. "Can't you give me a break? I thought it was a grouse. Honest."

Although Frostbow came across as sincere, Ed wasn't so sure he believed him. He had encountered more than a few outlaws in his long career who were skilled actors. Hen pheasants were protected year-round. Only the colorful males could be taken during the open pheasant season in Pennsylvania.

Ed said to him, "It's your responsibility to know what you're shooting at. You can take a hearing in front of a judge if you want but this is no mistake kill as far as I'm concerned."

Frostbow shook his head. "No sense in that. It's my mistake and I'm sure the judge will rule in your favor. Just write me a ticket and I'll pay."

Ed put the illegal kill in the trunk of his car and walked back to Frostbow a few minutes later with a handwritten citation for the violation.

"Mind if I ask a question?" Frostbow said as he slipped the ticket into his jacket pocket.

"Go ahead," Ed replied.

"Since I agreed to pay the fine, can I have my pheasant back?"

The sun dipped low on the horizon as Ed sat in his car by the UPS terminal, waiting for the driver who was supposed to return by three o'clock. But it wasn't until four-thirty that a brown delivery truck finally pulled into the parking lot.

Engine problems, explained the driver. His name was Ben.

Ed opened his trunk and showed him the box he'd found with the head and hide inside. Ben examined the tracking number on the label and went back to his truck to check his logbook. He returned a few minutes later with a smile on his face.

"The guy's name is Harry Harvey," he said. "Lives in Warminster. I delivered the box to him yesterday morning."

Ben scribbled an address on a notepad and tore the sheet off. "Hope you catch him," he said, handing the paper to Ed.

When Ed stepped up on Mr. Harvey's porch, he saw a carving knife lying by the front door, the blade encrusted with dried blood and deer hair. He knocked, hoping someone was home.

After a moment, the door swung open and a man with three days of stubble on his face gawked at him. He had long, stringy hair and wore a faded gray undershirt that stretched over a belly that swelled as if he were pregnant. His polka-dot pajama bottoms ended above his ankles. His feet were bare and his brown eyes were glassy and bloodshot from alcohol.

"Mr. Harvey?" Ed asked.

"That's right."

"I'm with the state game commission. I guess you know why I'm here."

Harvey's eyes flicked to the knife on the floor, then back to Ed. He nodded slowly. "It's about the deer, ain't it?"

"That's right."

"It was a roadkill," he said. "I picked it up yesterday afternoon. Brought it home and cut it up. Is that a problem?"

"It's against the law to do that."

Harvey looked surprised. "Why? It was lying by the road, dead as a doornail. I didn't shoot it or nothing like that."

Ed believed he was telling the truth. There were no holes or other markings in the hide that would indicate a bullet or an arrow had killed it. But still…

Ed said, "And after you cut it up, you put the head and hide in a box and dumped it in a field along Stump Road. Right?"

Harvey looked down at his bare toes and nodded.

"That's against the law, too. It's called littering."

"You gonna arrest me?" he asked, staring at his toes.

"I'm not going to put you in cuffs and haul you to jail if that's what you mean. But there is a fifty-dollar fine for the unlawful possession of the deer. And you'll have to turn the meat over to me."

Harvey jerked his head up in surprise. "Fifty dollars! That don't seem right. It was gonna be buzzard bait before I took it."

"I might agree with you if you hadn't dumped the head and hide by the road. Any idea what the county littering fine is?"

"No."

"Three hundred for incidents like yours."

Harvey let out a heavy sigh. "Are you gonna fine me for that, too?"

"No. This time it's just for the deer."

"I appreciate that," he said.

After collecting the venison from his freezer, Ed made arrangements to settle with him on a field acknowledgment of guilt later in the week.

"Got a second?" Harvey asked as Ed started to leave.

Ed turned to face him. "What is it?"

"You know, I always wanted a job like yours," he said. "Out in the woods, feeding the animals, breathing fresh air and stuff like that. Is the Game Commission hiring right now?"

The following October, Ed received word that Forrest Frostbow's hunting privileges had been revoked for killing the hen pheasant in January. A revocation notice was sent by certified mail but he refused to accept it; hence, it was returned to the Game Commission and subsequently forwarded to Ed for delivery in person.

Frostbow lived in a modest ranch-style brick-and-mortar home on a country road surrounded by a large tract of woods. A covered porch ran along the entire front. There were no immediate neighbors.

As Ed drove down a gravel driveway toward the house, he saw no vehicles on the property and suspected Frostbow might not be home.

After parking his sedan, he vaulted up on the porch and banged on the front door. Silence greeted him. No footfalls, no clatter of dishes, no TV noise, no radio music. The only sound was the wind rustling through the branches of nearby trees.

Thinking he'd stop back later in the day, Ed turned and started across the porch when a small copper-colored feather wedged between two floorboards caught his eye. He recognized it immediately as the breast feather of a male ring-necked pheasant.

Hunting season was closed, so Ed stepped off the porch and walked out to the backyard to look for Frostbow. The yard was empty save an old burn barrel sitting by the edge of the woods at the end of the property. Curious, he walked over for a closer look.

When he peered inside the barrel, he saw the charred remains of eight pheasants that had their breasts removed.

Lights glowed warmly through the windows of Frostbow's house as Ed's sedan crunched down the gravel driveway later that day. It was six o'clock in the evening, and Frostbow could hear the warden's car coming from inside his house. He stepped out on the porch as Ed approached the front door.

"Officer Bond," Frostbow said. "What brings you here?"

Ed withdrew a folded document from inside his uniform jacket. He handed it to Frostbow. "This comes directly from Harrisburg," he said. "It's your notice that your hunting privileges have been revoked for one year."

Frostbow unfolded the document and looked it over. "I knew this wasn't going to be a social visit when I saw you coming," he said glumly. "And I just bought my hunting license last week, too."

"You might as well go back inside and get it for me," Ed replied. "You won't be needing it for a while."

"You mean right now?"

"Purchasing a hunting license while on revocation is a violation."

"But I didn't know my license had been revoked."

"Well, now you do, so go get it for me."

Frostbow retreated into his house and returned a moment later with his license. He handed it to Ed. "Are we done now?"

"Afraid not."

"What, then?"

"I found the remains of eight pheasants in your burn barrel earlier today."

Frostbow paused, then looked over at the barrel as if to confirm it was still there. "Somebody gave them to me," he said. "I didn't kill them."

"Where are they?"

"I have four in my freezer. You're welcome to come in and see for yourself."

Ed followed Frostbow into the house and trailed him to the kitchen, where he retrieved four pheasant breasts wrapped in heavy paper from the freezer. Aside from a few steaks and frozen vegetables, nothing else was inside.

"Where are the other birds?" Ed asked."

"I'd rather not say."

"You have the remains of eight pheasants killed in closed season in your burn barrel. That puts you in violation eight times over—the same as if you'd killed them yourself."

Frostbow nodded that he understood. "How much is the fine?" he asked meekly.

Ed wanted to know who killed the birds and suspected he would never find out unless he made a deal with Frostbow.

"You're looking at a two-hundred-dollar fine," Ed told him (equal to two thousand dollars today).

Frostbow looked as if he'd just bitten into a lemon. "But I didn't even kill one single bird!"

"Tell me who did and I'll only charge you for two birds," Ed said. "Half of what was in your freezer."

Frostbow didn't have to think too long about the offer. "His name is Bob Dobbins," he said. "He works with me. He brought the birds over last week and we prepared them here. He said they were legal because he killed them on private property at his uncle's farm. I was stupid enough to believe him, too. He only lives a few miles from here."

Unlike Frostbow, Bob Dobbins lived in a rowhome in the suburbs of Philadelphia. After navigating a tangle of congested highways followed by an unending series of traffic lights, Ed Bond stepped up on Dobbins' front porch with a search warrant. It was late in the day, well after dark, when he knocked on the door.

He heard footsteps approaching from inside, then an overhead porch light bathed him in its glow.

"Who's there?" came a gruff voice from behind the door. It was male.

"State game commission," Ed said. "Open the door."

There was a prolonged pause. And as Ed began to fear he'd made the tedious drive to Philadelphia for nothing, the door creaked open just enough for someone to peek out at him.

"Mr. Dobbins?" Ed asked.

"Yes. What do you want?"

Ed reached into his jacket pocket and pulled out a folded document. He held it up so Dobbins could see it in the porch light.

"I have a search warrant for unlawfully killed game," Ed said, bracing his foot against the door to prevent it from closing.

"I don't know what you're talking about," Dobbins said. "What game?"

"The eight pheasants you killed and brought to Frostbow's house. Now step back and let me in."

"And if I don't?"

"I can have the Philadelphia Police Warrant Squad here in ten minutes. I'm sure you don't want that."

Ed thought it could be hours before they responded and hoped his ploy would work.

After a moment, Dobbins opened the door and invited Ed into a dimly lit living room. "You're right," he said. "I don't want those animals here."

Ed handed him a duplicate of the warrant. "This is your copy," he said. "It gives me the right to enter your house and search for illegal game."

Dobbins switched on an overhead light and examined the document carefully. In his mid-forties, with a wiry build, he had reddish hair combed back and a thin face, his lips set in a constant smirk.

"You're wasting your time with your search warrant," he said. "You won't find anything here."

Ed knew he might be telling the truth. Frostbow had told him the birds were killed a week ago. They could be long gone by now.

"I want to take a look in your freezer," Ed said.

Dobbins led him into the kitchen and pulled open the doors of both the refrigerator and the freezer. Frozen TV dinners and cans of beer were all that he found.

"Told you," Dobbins said. "You're wasting your time."

Ed checked the basement, thinking he might have a freezer there. He did not.

"I know what you did," Ed said to him after finishing his search and finding nothing. "Your buddy Forrest Frostbow told me all about it."

"Good luck with that," Dobbins scoffed. "It's his word against mine."

Ed knew Dobbins was right. Still, he filed charges against him based on the pheasants discovered in the burn barrel. Because Forrest Frostbow's testimony would be crucial at trial, Ed secured a subpoena from the justice of the peace, ordering him to appear in court.

In the 1960s, it seemed that anyone could become a justice of the peace. County residents elected them, and formal legal education was not necessary to qualify for the position. As a result, carpenters, plumbers, contractors, and various others presided over trials. During the day, they practiced their trades, and most legal proceedings took place at night. In the Dobbins case, the justice of the peace, or JP, was a full-time barber.

The JP sat in his barber's chair, surrounded by clumps of hair left by his last customer when Ed Bond walked through the door. He'd been running late due to heavy traffic. Forrest Frostbow, Bob Dobbins, and his lawyer had arrived shortly before him.

Seeing Ed, the JP spun his chair toward a polished wooden box of cigars on the table behind him. He plucked a thick cigar from the box, snipped the cap with a sharp guillotine cutter, and held a flaming wooden match to the opposite end. He puffed gently on the cigar until it produced a bright cherry-like glow. Turning back to Ed, he exhaled a cloud of gray smoke that swirled around his head, filling the room with its earthy aroma.

"Court is now in session," he proclaimed, and promptly stuck the cigar back into his mouth.

Ed called on Forrest Frostbow to testify, which prompted Dobbins' lawyer to immediately object on the grounds that he would incriminate himself if he said anything about the case.

Ed maintained that Frostbow had already pleaded guilty to possessing the pheasants and that he wouldn't bring any additional charges against him, anyway.

The two men argued back and forth at length, with neither of them giving an inch. Eventually, the JP became annoyed to the point that he spun his barber chair around, set his cigar in an ashtray behind him, and dismissed the case.

As Ed walked toward his car in the parking lot, Dobbins' attorney called out: "Officer Bond. Got a second?"

Ed turned and waited as he hustled over.

"How about that JP?" the attorney chuckled. "A real piece of work, huh?"

"He sure is," Ed agreed.

"You put up a good fight in there," he added. "I have to commend you for that."

Ed shrugged. "Win some, lose some."

The attorney smiled. "You really didn't lose tonight," he said in a low voice. "Dobbins is going to pay big time for my services, believe me."

Ed paused for a moment. "Why are you telling me this?"

"Because I envy you, man. I always wanted to be a forest ranger or a game warden." He folded his arms and looked into the middle distance. "But that chapter passed for me, and by the time I realized it, it was too late. I went to college and majored in criminal justice. Law school was next. Before I knew it, I was working for a big law firm in Philly. Now I'm defending dirtbags like Dobbins and looking back at my life, wondering where it all went. It's good money but I hate it."

Ed nodded in a way that told him he understood.

"As far as I'm concerned, you've got the greatest job in the world," the attorney said.

Ed smiled, his eyes crinkling with mischief. "You know, after all our arguing in court tonight, you finally said something we can agree on."

Up from the meadows rich with corn,
Clear in the cool September morn.
          ~John Greenleaf Whittier

THE BEST-LAID PLANS...

ARCHERY SEASON would soon open as Larry Lowlife trudged through the woods on that cool September morning with a burlap sack of corn slung over his shoulder. It was his third trip of the day, and he had been making similar visits for the past month. When he reached a clearing in the woods, he opened the sack and dumped its bright yellow kernels onto the ground.

He turned and gazed into the surrounding forest. It looked like a giant treasure chest had been opened, with mounds of gold piled as far as he could see. It was a beautiful sight to behold. A number of deer were feeding regularly on the corn and his multiple trail cameras, strategically placed at each bait pile, had recorded two trophy bucks and a dozen or more antlerless deer over the past weeks.

He had cleared a large section of the woods months ago by removing limbs from trees to create shooting lanes for his bow and later for his gun. Some of the smaller trees had been eliminated completely.

Larry planned to be in his treestand overlooking his secret treasure trove early on the first day of archery season. Then, after he had killed a nice buck and later a fat doe, he would invite his friends to hunt here. And they, in turn, would invite him to hunt the adjoining baited properties that ran along the Cumberland-Perry county line.

Finished for the day, Larry returned to his pickup truck parked on a dirt road a hundred yards away. Archery season would open in two weeks. Larry wasn't so sure he wanted to wait that long. After all, who would know?

Later that week, Game Warden Michael Smith was working on an anonymous tip about a large network of bait sites when he came upon the corn Larry Lowlife had been scattering throughout the forest. Michael noted that trail cameras monitored the area, a typical strategy of today's modern poacher. He also observed two treestands constructed where deer attracted to the bait could be targeted.

Although game wardens have their tricks to avoid trail cameras, which cannot be revealed here, there remained a chance that he might be captured on a hidden camera that he overlooked. With that thought in mind, the warden backtracked to his patrol vehicle, planning to return once more before opening day to familiarize himself with the area.

Later that afternoon, Michael contacted his neighboring officer, Rebecca Wolfe, and explained what he had found. The baited area was vast, covering her district in Cumberland County as well as his own in Perry County. After discussing the situation, they decided to work together, hoping to catch any poachers hunting in the area.

With only a few days remaining before the season opened, Michael and Rebecca returned to the baited forest to see if any new treestands had been set up.

The area was located at the summit of a mountain with only one way up. Their patrol car bounced along the steep, bumpy dirt road, dodging potholes and rocks until they reached the top and leveled out. After passing a swampy area, they parked behind a cluster of pine trees to conceal their vehicle.

Sunlight filtered through the branches of the trees, casting shaded patterns on the forest floor as they walked. The air was cool and crisp, filled with the scent of pine, damp soil, and decaying leaves.

After navigating dense brush and crawling over, under, and through numerous thorny briars, they finally reached a clearing in the woods. But when they arrived at the bait pile Michael had discovered earlier, all that remained were bare dirt and scattered crumbs.

Determined to push on, they split up to cover more ground in less time. Michael traveled east while Rebecca searched north, but it appeared that the poachers had deserted the area, as the corn that had been there earlier was gone. The deer had cleaned out the bait, leaving no trace behind.

Michael and Rebecca returned to their starting point to discuss their findings, or lack thereof, while staying behind the trail cameras that were still awake and watching.

That's when Rebecca heard the subtle snap of a branch breaking in the distance, alerting them that something was approaching.

Michael's eyes widened as he followed Rebecca's gaze toward the sound, expecting to see a bear or a huge buck deer.

Instead, they saw a man approaching. He was only fifty yards away, heading straight for them, his gaze fixed on the ground as he advanced. The wardens crouched low, hoping not to be discovered as they whispered plans for a hasty retreat.

Rebecca thought they might be able to sneak out of sight if they moved quickly and stepped lightly, but the woods were open and the odds were stacked against them.

The faint crunch of leaves underfoot grew louder as he neared. Soon, he was only fifteen feet away, eyes still on the ground, a bulging burlap sack over his right shoulder.

The wardens crouched low and watched as he opened his sack and spilled twenty-five pounds of feed corn onto the ground. And when they suddenly stood and identified themselves, Larry Lowlife jumped three feet into the air.

Although they couldn't charge him for hunting over bait, he was cited for feeding deer within a deer management area where Chronic Wasting Disease had been detected.

Rebecca and Michael returned to the baited area several times throughout the season but never found any poachers. Apparently, the word had spread like wildfire that game wardens were patrolling the property.

As the saying goes, the best-laid plans of mice and men (and women) often go awry. After all, who could have known on a Thursday afternoon before hunting season that a suspected poacher would nearly trip over two game wardens hidden in the brush?

Rebecca and Michael still laugh about it to this day, but next time, they promise to be as quick as the wind so they can catch a poacher without getting caught themselves.

Injustice is relatively easy to bear; what stings is justice.
   ~Henry Louis Mencken

CITY BOYS

HARLEY WINKLER and Sneed McLumpski were hunting buddies with bad reputations. They showed no regard for seasons or bag limits and would kill a deer any time they had the chance. Ed Bond had heard rumors about them for years. They were an elusive pair who managed to cover their tracks well, and tips about their poaching activities were always too little and too late. But things finally changed when he received an anonymous tip that they had killed a nice buck and were headed back to Philadelphia with the carcass.

His informant had given him a description of their car and the license number. It led to an address on Division Street in Northeast Philadelphia.

Ed Bond drove into the city, hot on their trail. It was a September morning in 1973. Hunting season was closed, and he hoped to catch them in possession of the deer before they could cut it up and dispose of the carcass.

Tall buildings towered above, their shadows cloaking the streets as Ed navigated the bustling city traffic. He dodged delivery trucks and lumbering Greyhound buses for nearly an hour before arriving at the quiet dead-end street where Harley Winkler lived.

He turned in and brought his vehicle to a crawl while scanning the street numbers posted on each front door of the thirty homes connected by shared sidewalls, known as rowhomes. Midway down the street, he spotted the address he was looking for. Winkler's black 1969 Ford Fairlane was parked among a long line of cars on the narrow street. Ed was fortunate to find a spot to squeeze his vehicle between two cars a few doors from his suspect.

Bond strode across the street and mounted three steps onto a small front porch. He rapped on the door, hoping to catch the poacher with blood on his hands.

After a moment, the door creaked open and a frail elderly woman looked up at him. Her gray hair bristled with pink rollers.

"State Game Commission," Ed announced. "I'm here to see Harley Winkler."

"I'm afraid you have the wrong house," she replied in a thin voice. She pointed a bony finger at the homes across the street and said, "He lives over there. The house with the green front door."

Ed didn't know if the address from the police database was wrong or if the dispatcher had mistakenly transposed the house number. He apologized and thanked the woman for pointing him in the right direction. Then he quickly descended her porch steps and went across the street to the house with the green door.

He knocked, and when no one answered he glanced over his shoulder at the Ford parked along the street to confirm that it was Winkler's car. Certain it was, Ed couldn't help but think he was hiding inside. He rapped on the door once more, louder this time. Again, there was no response, so he circled the block on foot and went down the back alley to see if Winkler had cellar windows at the rear of his house that would reveal the illegal deer.

The alley was a narrow ribbon of asphalt, allowing passage solely for pedestrians or bicycles. Steel trash cans, black iron gas pipes, and metal utility meters flanked the exterior walls of the weathered red brick homes. Air conditioning units protruded from the upper windows, but the smaller lower windows were unobstructed, offering basement views. But when he reached Winkler's house, the windows were curtained, preventing a peek inside.

Convinced that Harley Winkler was home, Ed quickly jogged back around the block to Division Street just in time to see Winkler's car speeding toward him. He did a double take when he saw Sneed McLumpski sitting on the trunk, gripping both fenders by his fingertips.

"There goes my deer!" Ed thought and ran after the car as it shot past him toward Conrad Street.

But city traffic had backed up at the intersection, causing Winkler to stop and wait for an opening, allowing Ed to catch up to them.

Just as Winkler began to nose his car into the flow, Bond reached through the open window of the driver's door and grabbed hold of the steering wheel with his left hand.

"State game warden!" he shouted. *"Stop!"*

Winkler looked straight ahead, pulling onto Conrad Street as Ed ran alongside the car.

Sneed McLumpski's eyes grew wide when he saw Ed reach down with his right hand and grip his holstered revolver.

"Stop, or I'll shoot out your tires!" Ed warned. He wouldn't have but it sounded good at the time.

"Do what he says, Harley!" McLumpski screamed in panic. "He's got a gun!"

Winkler whipped his head around and eyeballed Ed, a mixture of fear and panic in his eyes. "Don't shoot! I'm stopping right now."

It was a good thing, too, because McLumpski was beginning to slide off the trunk, holding on desperately. If Winkler had continued driving, his friend could have been seriously injured or killed by falling onto the road.

After pulling to the curb, Winkler shut off his engine and stared at Ed Bond in silence.

Ed ordered Winkler out of the Ford. He eyed him carefully as Winkler pushed open the driver's door and slipped out.

"Step to the back of the car," Bond commanded. His tone was sharp.

Winkler did as he was told. McLumpski slid off the trunk and stood beside him while passing motorists blasted their horns and shook their fists in frustration as they steered around his car and inched down Conrad Street toward the inner city.

Harley Winkler had a stocky build with a balding head, shifty eyes, and a scruffy black beard. Sneed McLumpski was tall and thin with ginger hair and a wispy blonde mustache. Both men were in their early forties.

"I know you killed a deer this morning," Ed said. "It was a buck. I want you to open your trunk."

"I don't know what you're talking about," said Winkler.

McLumpski shifted his weight nervously from one foot to the other and stared at Ed with eyes like saucers.

"Got a warrant?" Winkler asked.

"No, but I can get one," Ed said, knowing how utterly impossible that would be in Philadelphia.

"Go ahead," Winkler said with a telling smile. "I'll wait right here."

Sneed McLumpski looked like he was about to throw up. He was the weak link and Ed needed to take advantage of it.

Ed said to McLumpski, "I can see deer hair and blood on the bumper of your friend's car. I know there's a deer in the trunk and that you were sitting on it to conceal evidence. That puts you in even more trouble than Mr. Winkler."

McLumpski swallowed hard. "What kind of trouble?"

"Shut up!" barked Winkler. "He's bluffing."

Ed said, "I'll tell you what kind of trouble: a hundred-dollar fine for the deer in addition to resisting inspection and aiding and abetting a game law violator. Those charges carry a nine-hundred-dollar fine."

Ed paused to let the implications of what he'd said settle in. Then: "But I can forget about those additional charges if you cooperate and tell me about the deer."

McLumpski looked at Winkler, his face pained. "I ain't got that kind of money, Harley."

Ed turned to Winkler. "Same goes for you. I know there's a deer in your trunk. Fess up and it'll be one charge for you as well."

Winkler thought for a moment, then heaved a deep sigh. "No sense fighting this," he said. "You got us."

He pulled a ring of keys from the pocket of his jeans and unlocked the trunk. "Hope it doesn't go to waste," he muttered as he lifted the lid.

A medium-sized four-point buck lay on its side, a .30 caliber bullet hole visible behind its left shoulder. The deer had been gutted, its hide still intact. A Marlin Model 336 lever action rifle rested by the carcass.

"I have a deer rack attached to the back of my car," Ed said to both men. "Take the deer and load it on the rack."

Passing motorists stopped briefly to stare as Winkler and McLumpski each took one end of the carcass and carried it to the back of Ed's patrol car. They placed it on the aluminum rack and stepped back while Ed secured it with rubber bungee cords.

After securing the carcass, he turned to face the men.

"Who shot the deer?" he asked.

"I did," Winkler admitted.

"Did you use the rifle that's in your trunk?"

Winkler nodded.

"I'll be taking it with me then."

"That's my father's gun. He willed it to me. You can't take that."

"It's evidence," Ed said.

Winkler stared at him, lips pursed into a pouting frown, eyes misty. He looked pitiful.

Ed couldn't help but feel a tinge of empathy for the guy. "I'll tell you what," he said. "Meet me next Saturday at the state police barracks in Limerick. If you plead guilty on a field acknowledgment and pay your fine, I'll have your rifle waiting for you."

Winkler heaved a sigh of relief. "Thanks, man," he said. "That means a lot to me."

"Just don't let me catch you doing this again," Ed told him. "Next time, you won't get it back."

"Harley Winkler raised his palms in a gesture of submission. "Don't worry," he said. "Sneed and me are done poaching deer forever."

The following year, Ed ran into them again.

Harley Winkler eased his 1969 Ford along a desolate back road in Solebury Township as Sneed McLumpski sat in the passenger seat, shining a spotlight into a wide grassy field. It was two o'clock in the morning, the air chilly under a bright October moon.

"There's one!" Sneed breathed. "Stop the car!"

A lonely doe grazed in the field fifty yards away, the spotlight illuminating its tawny coat while casting deep shadows behind it.

Winkler wheeled his Ford to the edge of the road, cut off the lights and killed the engine.

The doe raised her head and looked toward them, her tail held high.

"She's ready to run," Winkler said in a low voice. "Keep the light on her. It's an easy shot as long as she stays put."

Winkler eased open the driver's door and slipped out with his Marlin rifle. The Ford's interior light had been disabled, so the poachers were concealed in darkness even though the door was wide open. Winkler leaned over the hood of his car, pointed the barrel of his rifle at the doe, and eased his index finger against the trigger.

At that moment, Sneed McLumpski sneezed, his spotlight recoiling in his grip as Winkler was about to pull the trigger.

The deer suddenly bolted, racing toward a distant bank of trees.

Harley Winkler watched in dismay as the spotlight's beam flashed across the field, left to right. He cursed under his breath as he stood and shouldered his rifle for a quick shot.

Kapow!

He missed.

McLumpski quickly found the deer in his light but sneezed again, causing the beam to bounce wildly across the treetops. By the time he regained his composure, the deer was gone.

Winkler marched over to the open driver's door and glared at his partner. "Nice going, Sneed," he said bitterly. "We finally see a deer and you fall into a sneezing frenzy."

But Sneed never looked at him. Instead, he sat rigidly in his seat, pointing through the windshield, his mouth moving a hundred miles an hour without uttering a word.

Winkler swung his head around and stared into the gloom of night.

He saw flashing red lights approaching. And they were coming fast.

Harley Winkler raised his hands in the air as he faced the police vehicle that had stopped in front of him. Sneed McLumpski sat frozen with fear inside the Ford as two Solebury Township police officers exited their vehicle.

Approaching a suspect's car from the front is never a good idea. But the officers left their headlights on, blinding both suspects as they moved toward them with guns drawn.

"Keep your hands in the air," a gruff voice cautioned behind the lights. Winkler squinted against the glare, barely able to see the two uniformed officers as they approached.

When they reached the front bumper, they split up. One walked off to check the passenger inside while the other approached Winkler and extracted a set of handcuffs from his duty belt.

As he snapped the cuffs on his suspect, he glanced into the car and spotted a rifle on the seat.

"Gun!" he hollered.

The second officer pointed his revolver directly at McLumpski inside the car, still clutching his spotlight.

"Get out of the car, now!" he shouted.

McLumpski stared at the gun leveled at him. The gaping black muzzle seemed as big as a cannon. Paralyzed with fear, he couldn't move, but the officer mistook his panic for stubbornness.

"I'm not going to tell you again!" the officer cried. "Keep your hands in the air and get out of the car. Do not make any sudden movements."

McLumpski summoned all his will to open the door, then stepped out slowly, arms raised, palms open.

"Turn around," ordered the officer.

McLumpski complied, and the officer holstered his firearm before handcuffing him. Then he escorted him to the front of the Ford, shoulder to shoulder with Harley Winkler.

When the officers realized that their suspects were not planning to burglarize homes but instead were suspected poachers, they seized their rifle and spotlight, took down the necessary information from their driver's licenses and turned the information over to Ed Bond the following day.

Deputy Ray Vees accompanied Ed Bond when he returned to Philadelphia weeks later with arrest warrants for Winkler and McLumpski. Both men had failed to respond to the citations filed against them for the incident in Solebury Township. Deputy Vees was in plain clothes as he knocked on Winkler's front door. It was late in the evening and well after dark.

Bond had parked his patrol car out of sight and was standing on the darkened porch out of view in full uniform. He didn't want a repeat performance from a year earlier when Winkler had fled in his car.

"Who's there?" a voice called from inside.

Vees said, "If that's your '69 Ford Fairlane parked on the street, I just backed into it."

When Vees saw the doorknob start to turn, he glanced at Ed with a sharp nod.

Concerned about the damage to his car, Winkler swung open the door. Vees immediately jammed his foot against it so it couldn't close.

"State Game Commission!" he stated firmly. "We have a warrant for your arrest."

Ed Bond quickly appeared alongside his deputy and ordered Winkler to move away from the door.

"What's this all about?" cried Winkler as he stepped back. He was dressed only in his underwear.

Both wardens shouldered past him into the house and shut the door behind them. Ed handed Winkler a copy of the warrant. "You're under arrest for attempting to kill a deer in closed season."

"What deer? What are you talking about?"

"About a month ago," Ed replied. "Solebury Township. You and McLumpski."

Winkler offered a dismissive wave of his hand. "Yeah, yeah, I remember," he said. "That's bogus, man. There was another car spotlighting that night. They shot at the deer and took off right before the cops came. I told them about it but they didn't believe me."

"I don't believe you, either," Ed said. "But I brought a citation with me, and I can let you go if you sign it and pay the fine in cash as collateral. I'll return the citation and the money to the judge in Bucks County and he'll set a hearing date. You'll get your money back if you're found not guilty."

"Huh!" Winkler scoffed. "Sounds like a shakedown to me."

"Your only other choice is to go to jail tonight."

"I ain't going nowhere with you. You guys just broke into my house, and I'm calling the cops."

Ed checked his watch, then said, "I saved you the trouble and called them myself half an hour ago. They should be here about now."

Deputy Vees opened the front door and looked out at the street.

"Yep," he said. "They just pulled up in a paddy wagon."

Harley Winkler backed into a corner of the room, eyes bulging as two Philadelphia police officers in blue uniforms stepped through the door.

Ed thanked them for coming and presented the arrest warrant for Winkler.

"Is that him?" one asked, chinning toward Winkler.

Ed nodded that it was.

"Put some clothes on," the officer said. "You're coming with us."

Winkler shook his head. "You want me, you're gonna have to take me as I am."

Ed didn't understand why Winkler had challenged them. Perhaps he thought they would refuse to arrest him dressed only in his underwear. If that was the case, it backfired. Both cops were on him in a flash. They quickly handcuffed Winkler and whisked him out the door and into the paddy wagon without looking back.

"Stay with us," one of the officers called to Ed over his shoulder. We'll see you at the Roundhouse."

Pennsylvania Rules of Criminal Procedure required police officers to bring defendants before the nearest on-duty magistrate when serving arrest warrants after six o'clock in the evening. Winkler would have to be brought before a Philadelphia judge before being transported out of the city.

It was standard procedure for the Game Commission to have the Philadelphia police assist whenever game wardens served warrants in the city. Working in Philadelphia was like operating in a different universe and presented unique challenges, including travel through congested city streets. Even while in full uniform and driving an officially marked patrol car, game wardens were often not recognized as law enforcement officers by many city residents, including some judges and police officers.

Ed and his deputy followed the two police officers and their shackled prisoner into the ground-floor entrance of the Roundhouse. In those days, it served as the headquarters for the Philadelphia Police Department, where justice was administered in the city. Before entering the area where prisoners were held, all four officers handed their guns over to a guard, who placed them in individual metal safety lockers that could only be opened with a combination of random numbers.

The guard unlocked a steel door that led to a large room where more than a dozen prisoners were held in a chamber at the far corner. The front of the chamber was sealed with Plexiglas. Several guards monitored the prisoners, who could see both the guards and anyone entering the area. When Harley Winkler was escorted into the room wearing only his underwear, it prompted open laughter, whistling, and catcalling from the prisoners. For his protection, he was kept outside the chamber.

Ed and his deputy waited for an hour before all the prisoners, shackled in leg irons, were escorted up a long flight of steps into a spacious courtroom. They followed the line of chained men into the room and waited until the judge finished with several other cases before he called the wardens to his bench.

The judge studied Ed's uniform as he approached. "What agency are you with?" he asked. Apparently, he'd never seen a uniformed game warden before.

"I'm with the Pennsylvania Game Commission," Ed told him. He explained the circumstances under which he'd brought in Harley Winkler.

After reviewing the arrest warrant, the judge arranged for a Philadelphia police officer to escort the wardens and their prisoner out of the city to the Bucks County boundary line. Along the way, they stopped at Winkler's house to pick up some clothing to wear while he was incarcerated.

Harley Winkler spent the night in a Solebury Township jail cell until Ed Bond came for him the following morning and brought him before the local district justice. Winkler looked like he hadn't slept a wink and decided he would plead guilty to the poaching charges. He asked to be placed on a payment plan, and the judge granted his request. Winkler called Sneed McLumpski to explain what happened and asked for a ride back to Philadelphia. With no desire to endure the same ordeal as Winkler, Sneed arrived at the judge's office an hour later and pleaded guilty to the poaching charges against him as well.

"Are we done meeting like this?" Ed asked both men before they left for Philadelphia.

Winkler nodded solemnly. "I'll never poach another deer again. I have finally learned my lesson."

"Fair enough," Ed said.

"I do have one question, however."

"Shoot," Ed said, immediately wishing he hadn't used the term.

"When do I get my rifle back? The cops took it when they swooped in on us that night."

"Not this time, Harley," Ed said. "I told you last year that you wouldn't get it back if I caught you poaching again."

Winkler steepled his fingers in a gesture of prayer. "But I promise, warden, Sneed and me are done poaching forever. You have my word."

"I don't believe you, Harley. You can't help yourself. It's like a sickness with you. You're not getting your rifle back."

"But it belonged to my father."

"You should have thought about that before you tried to jacklight another deer."

Winkler hung his head and sighed. "Please, warden, I'm begging you."

Once again, Ed couldn't help but feel sorry for the guy, even if he was a poacher. Relenting, he told him about the Game Commission auction, held annually in Harrisburg for confiscated equipment (the practice has been discontinued). He said that he knew of people who had bid on their confiscated firearms to get them back.

Winkler thanked him for the information, a glimmer of hope in his eyes.

There was no doubt in Ed's mind that Winkler and McLumpski would be at it again. Since Harley Winkler had been operating primarily in Solebury Township, Ed needed a way to communicate directly with the police to even the odds of catching them in the act. Later that same week, he installed a police scanner in his patrol car. He did this at his own expense and set it on the police radio frequency. Several police departments also had the Game Commission frequency in their cars. Solebury was one of them.

Ed started spending more time patrolling at night, and several weeks later, a Solebury Police car reported that it had stopped Sneed McLumpski. He had been cruising slowly along Greenhill Road at two in the morning. The officers knew that if McLumpski was in the area, Winkler had to be nearby.

Bond was only a few miles away, parked on a windswept ridge watching over a broad valley below for poachers. Pleased that his idea about scanners had paid off, he keyed the ignition and hurried toward Greenhill Road.

As Ed accelerated down the dark country road, a large doe suddenly materialized, its pale yellow eyes illuminated by his headlights. It stood motionless in the center of the road. Ed slammed on the brakes, his tires screeching wildly against the asphalt. Then, just as swiftly as the deer had appeared, it vanished without a trace. Ed exhaled sharply, his heart hammering in his chest. Relieved that no harm had come to the doe, he couldn't help but find it ironic that he'd nearly struck one of the very creatures he'd sworn to protect from the poacher's gun.

Patrolman Jim Slade and Corporal Tom Whitmore stood between McLumpski's battered Chevy and their patrol car as Ed drove by and made a three-point turn and parked behind them.

Ed exited his car and strode over to the three men, nodding a hello to the officers.

"He had a loaded rifle with him," Corporal Whitmore said to Ed. "We have it in our car."

Ed nodded. "No surprise."

He turned to McLumpski. "Where is your buddy, Harley?"

"He ain't here," he responded. "I told the officers when they stopped me, I was just out driving around, that's all."

"I'll tell you what *I* think," Ed said. "I think you dropped off Winkler somewhere after he shot a deer and he's out there waiting for you to pick him up."

McLumpski shook his head no. "Like I said, I was just out driving around. Is that illegal?"

"It is when you have a loaded rifle in your car."

"But I didn't know it was loaded."

"That's no excuse," Ed said. "But you've got bigger issues to worry about: if Winkler killed a deer, you're going to face the same charges as he does. Tell me where you dropped him off and I'll give you a break."

"What kind of a break?"

"I won't have the police take you to jail tonight. How's that sound?"

McLumpski hugged himself and stared at his boots as he considered his options. After a long moment, he looked up at Ed. "Honest, I don't know where he is," he said. "I got lost after I dropped him off. I was driving around looking for him when the cops stopped me."

"He shot a deer, didn't he," Ed said.

"Yup."

"I'll tell you what we're going to do," Ed said. "You're going to get back in your car and start driving until we find him. I'll be in the back seat to make sure you don't get lost again."

Ed looked at Whitmore and Slade. "Can you hang with me for a while?"

"Wouldn't miss it for the world," Corporal Whitmore said. "We'll be patrolling the area as well. With luck, we might run into him."

As Ed slid into the back seat of McLumpski's car, the corporal gave him a hand-held police radio so they could stay in touch.

Half an hour later, Ed received a radio call from Corporal Whitmore saying that Winkler had flagged down their police vehicle, thinking it was McLumpski. They were holding him on Stagecoach Road.

Ed ordered McLumpski to stop the car. The moment it came to a halt, he leaned over the back seat and yanked the keys out of the ignition. Then he leaped out of the car and flung open the driver's door.

"Move over," he said. "It's my turn to drive."

Ed slid behind the wheel and hit the gas. Stagecoach Road was close by; they arrived within minutes.

Ed parked behind the police vehicle and instructed McLumpski to remain in place. He swung out of the car and moved to Winkler and the two patrol officers.

"Let me see your hands," he said to Winkler.

Winkler did as he was told. Ed clicked on his Maglite and found dried blood on his fingers and inside his nails.

"Where is the deer?" Ed said.

Winkler looked at him, his face a mix of defiance and regret, not for poaching a deer, but regret for getting caught.

Winkler shrugged. "What deer?"

Ed wasn't in the mood for playing games and walked away without saying another word. He knew the deer had to be nearby since this was where Winkler had flagged down the police. After a brief search of the adjacent woods, Ed found a gutted doe and dragged it back to the road.

In the end, Harley Winkler and Sneed McLumpski admitted to hunting after hours and illegally killing a whitetail deer. They were each fined hundreds of dollars and had their hunting licenses suspended for an extended period of time.

In the following years, reports surfaced that Winkler continued to poach deer. Ed visited his home in Philadelphia to investigate but found that Winkler no longer lived there. He spoke to several neighbors and the current residents of Winkler's house. No one knew where he was. One person suggested that he might have moved to New Jersey.

If true, he must have taken McLumpski with him, for Ed Bond never saw Harley Winkler or Sneed McLumpski again.

He can run, but he can't hide.
～Joe Louis

GUT SHOT

I<small>T WAS THE LAST DAY</small> of buck season in 1999 when Deputy Game Warden Jeff Pierce had another run-in with the McCoys. In those days, you could only shoot antlered deer during a two-week firearms season in Pennsylvania, which was immediately followed by a three-day antlerless deer season.

Jeff had dropped off his son-in-law, Paul, before daylight at a place they called the Thirty-Acre Field. Paul had seen a trophy buck in the area and wanted one last chance to take it before doe season opened the following Monday.

Jeff wished Paul good luck and proceeded to make his way through the mountains of Wyoming County, patrolling the southeastern part of his district.

Hunting pressure had been light that day, so after ten hours of patrol without any cell phone calls from his son-in-law, Jeff drove back to the Thirty-Acre Field and parked along the dirt road where he had dropped Paul off that morning.

The sun was slowly melting into the horizon when he saw Paul coming toward him through the field a hundred yards away. Anxious to hear about his day, Jeff exited his patrol vehicle and walked out to meet him.

"See anything?" Jeff asked as they met.

"Heard some distant shots earlier," Paul replied, "but I didn't see brown until about fifteen minutes ago when I jumped a doe on my way back."

"Doe season starts Monday," Jeff said. "Maybe you'll see it again and get a good shot off."

"Hope so," Paul said. "Let's head back. It's getting close to dinner time and I'm starved."

From out of nowhere, the sound of a rifle shot rolled across the field, shattering the tranquil evening.

Paul recoiled. "*Wow!* That was close. I bet someone just shot that doe I saw."

"Wait here," Jeff said. "I'll go check it out."

Jeff jumped into his patrol vehicle and drove to the other side of the field, where he saw a white Dodge Ram pickup truck standing. Jeff shut off his headlights, pulled in behind the truck, and parked.

Moments later, he observed the silhouettes of two armed hunters approaching in the dim light of dusk. He stayed in his unmarked truck until they were close, then stepped out in full uniform. Jeff recognized one of the hunters as Liam McCoy, whose uncle owned a local butcher shop that processed deer.

"State game warden!" Jeff announced. "Who fired that shot?"

McCoy's hunting partner immediately turned and fled, disappearing into the moonless night before Jeff could get a good look at him.

Liam McCoy continued toward Jeff, stepping within handshaking distance. "Deputy Pierce!" he said. "Didn't realize it was you."

"It's me all right," Jeff said. "Who was the guy that just took off?"

Liam shrugged innocently. "I don't know. "He was coming out of the woods about the same time as me and we just started walking out together."

Jeff was too familiar with the McCoys and their schemes to believe he was telling the truth.

"Don't lie to me, Liam. Who was he?"

"He never told me his name, honest," said Liam. "I've got no idea."

Jeff extended his right hand and Liam reached out to grasp his palm.

Jeff shook his head. "I want your rifle, not a handshake."

Liam rolled his eyes as he withdrew his hand and surrendered his Ruger bolt action rifle.

Jeff opened the action and slid out a live round before putting the muzzle to his nose. "Hasn't been fired all day," he said. "So I guess it was the mystery man who took the late shot."

"Late?" Liam questioned.

"It was dark," Jeff said. "Legal hunting hours ended at sunset."

Jeff handed back his rifle. "If I find out that you know this guy and he shot a deer, you're going to be prosecuted right along with him."

"What are you talking about, man? I didn't do anything."

"That's the problem," Jeff said, poker-faced.

"Huh?"

"It's called aiding and abetting. If you're protecting him, that makes you an accomplice. Plain and simple. Tell me who he is and you won't be charged with anything."

"Like I said, I don't know the guy."

Jeff realized he was getting nowhere and was growing concerned about his son-in-law, whom he had left on the other side of the field. "Turn around so I can check your hunting license," he said to Liam.

Liam did as he was told. Jeff pulled the cardboard license from its plastic holder pinned to the back of his hunting coat. Liam's address was listed as Ridley Street in Philadelphia. All of the big game tags were in place, indicating he hadn't shot a buck—or if he had, he failed to tag it as required by law.

Jeff said, "You didn't drive all the way from Philadelphia just to turn around and go home tonight, did you?"

"No."

"You must be staying with your uncle, Connor McCoy, then, right?"

He nodded that he was.

"Good," Jeff said. "I'll know where to find you."

Jeff found his son-in-law walking home in the dark on a narrow country road and stopped to pick him up. Paul was glad to see him; he'd been out in the cold all day and wasn't looking forward to the two-mile trek back to his house.

"How'd you make out?" Paul asked as he slid into the passenger seat and switched the heater to high.

"I ran into Liam McCoy and another hunter coming back to their truck," Jeff said as he wheeled down the road. "The other guy ran when he saw me."

"Recognize him?"

"No. Never got a good look at him."

"Think he was the one who fired the shot?"

"Yes," Jeff said. "Nobody else was around and Liam was nervous when I questioned him. Said he didn't know the guy, even though they were walking side by side when I saw them."

"So now what?"

"After I drop you off, I'll go back out there to look around. They may have killed or wounded a deer."

The stars were bright and hard, illuminating the meadow as he approached. Seventy yards out, he saw her clearly under their glow; the only sound was the steady crunch of his leather boots as he moved toward her.

The doe stood in the grassy field with her head low. Her intestines spilled from a wound in her belly, glistening like an uncoiled serpent. She didn't try to run when she heard him coming. Didn't move a muscle.

When he was close, he drew his revolver from its holster, the worn leather creaking softly as it came free.

The doe lifted her heavy head and stared at him with unblinking eyes as if waiting for him to end her misery.

He pointed his gun at her heart and slowly squeezed the trigger.

Liam McCoy stood there with three of his poaching buddies when Jeff Pierce walked into the butcher shop unannounced an hour later. All the men except one wore coveralls that were bloody and stained from processing deer. Like Liam, he was in his twenties and stood out from the others in his clean white coveralls.

Jeff noticed the scratches and cuts on his face and hands, most likely from running through the woods when he'd fled earlier. Jeff stared at him critically and the man quickly dropped his eyes. There was no doubt in Jeff's mind that this was the person who had been with Liam before.

The property owner, Connor McCoy, a bearish man with a great red beard and piercing green eyes, pointed at the door. "You can turn around and walk right back out the door you came in," he grunted. "You got no business here and I want you off my property."

Jeff said, "A doe was shot in the Thirty-Acre Field tonight. Your nephew and his buddy over there with the clean coveralls were both involved."

Connor turned toward Liam. "Is that true?" His voice was harsh.

Liam looked terrified. Jeff suspected he was more afraid of his uncle than anyone else. "I don't know anything about it, Uncle," he said. "I heard a shot but I don't know where it came from."

Thinking Liam would like nothing more than to be away from Connor McCoy at that moment, Jeff took advantage of the situation.

"Why don't you step outside with me, Liam?" he said. "I have a few questions for you."

"Do what he asks," his uncle told him. "And you better not have brought trouble into my shop."

Liam followed Jeff out the door and walked with him across the small parking lot until they reached Jeff's pickup truck parked by Liam's Dodge Ram.

Jeff stepped around to the back of his truck and dropped the tailgate, exposing the doe that had been shot earlier.

"I had to finish her off," Jeff said, shaking his head to add weight to the burden. "Nothing worse than having your guts blown out by some idiot who can't shoot."

Liam gave a helpless shrug. "Guess so."

Jeff said, "Who's the guy with the clean coveralls? I recognized everybody in the shop but him."

"Name's Jim."

"Jim who?"

"Why can't you leave me alone, man?" Liam moaned. "I don't want to rat on him. He's a friend."

"I tried to explain this before," Jeff said. "If you're not part of the solution, you're part of the problem. If you remain part of the problem, I'm going to write you up for a bunch of fines." Jeff paused so Liam could think about what he'd just said. Then: "Do you want to be part of the problem, Liam?"

Liam shook his head no.

"Good. Now what is Jim's last name?"

Liam looked over at the butcher shop, then back to Jeff. "Shimko," he said. "Jim Shimko."

"Where is his gun?"

"It's not *his* gun," Liam said. "It's my father's. I loaned it to him."

"Where is it?"

"It's in my truck."

"Let's go get it."

I was completing an investigation in the northwestern corner of my four-hundred-square-mile district when Jeff Pierce contacted me by radio. He asked me to meet him at the Exeter Township Police Station for an interview with two suspected poachers.

I grabbed the mic from its clip on the dashboard and put it to my face. *"Ten-four. I'll head over there right now."*

Exeter Township lies at the southern end of Wyoming County, and it took me about half an hour to reach the police station. I pulled into the parking lot and parked my car. A heavy cloud cover had rolled in, obscuring the stars that had shone so brightly earlier in the night. The parking lot felt dark and bleak. It was illuminated by a single overhead streetlight that hummed at me as I walked across the asphalt into the station.

A police officer wearing a nickel-plated name tag engraved with "WILKINS" greeted me. He looked to be in his early twenties.

"He's in the interrogation room," he said, nodding toward a long cinderblock hallway that was painted beige. "Last door on the right. He's got two suspects with him."

I thanked him and started down the hallway when he called out.

"Warden...?"

I stopped and turned toward him.

"I was wondering if the Game Commission was hiring right now?"

"Sorry," I said, "but they started a class last summer. It'll probably be two or three years before the next one."

His mouth tightened and he nodded grimly. "I'd like to be a game warden one day," he said. "Maybe next time."

I smiled supportively. "Get a subscription to *Pennsylvania Game News*," I offered. "They'll announce the next class far in advance. You'll enjoy the magazine, too. Lots of good hunting stories."

"Thank you, sir," he said. "I'll do that. And good luck with those two poachers back there. Hope you nail them to the wall."

I nodded and started down the dimly lit hallway, passing several empty offices and a lunchroom. I had an excellent relationship with the state police at the time and would often stop by with a handful of *Pennsylvania Game News* magazines to leave in the lunchroom. I made a mental note to start doing the same for the township police officers in my district.

Jeff Pierce sat in the interview room with Liam McCoy and Jim Shimko when I walked through the open doorway. His two suspects knew we had to prove they shot a deer in closed season and that we had no eyewitness who could testify against them. I suspected both men realized they had an advantage over us. But the fact that they were sitting there with my deputy gave me hope that I'd get a confession from at least one of them.

Jeff was dressed in his uniform: a tan shirt with a silver badge on his chest, forest green pants, polished black boots, and a leather holster equipped with a .357 Magnum revolver. The same uniform I wore. Liam McCoy and Jim Shimko were dressed in jeans, canvas shirts, and Carhart work boots. Liam was tall and broad-shouldered. He had red hair and dark green eyes like his uncle, Connor McCoy. Shimko was tall and thin, almost gaunt, with sandy-colored hair that fell to his collar. He had a square jaw and dark brown eyes with flecks of gold. His eyes never stopped moving from Liam to Jeff and back to me, only to start over again as he sat on the edge of his chair.

I signaled Jeff to follow me into the hallway. Out of earshot from the suspects, he briefed me on the events.

"Ask Officer Wilkins to put on a pot of coffee," I said. "Looks like it's going to be a long night."

Since Shimko was fidgeting in his chair and scanning the room with his eyes as if searching for a way to escape, I figured he was the weak link. McCoy looked calm, and from what Jeff had told me earlier, he was a career poacher. I'd probably have to beat a confession out of him. Although the idea was appealing, I quickly shook it out of my head and asked Jeff to escort him out of the room.

When we were alone, I slid an empty straight-backed chair directly in front of Shimko, hoping he wouldn't suspect my scheme to get him to confess.

"Mind if I sit down?" I said as I plopped into my seat. We were so close that our knees almost touched.

Shimko pulled his chest back and straightened in his chair.

"You know what?" I said, leaning into him, "I'm a hunter just like you. I know what it's like to be out there on the last day of buck season with nothing to show for it but cold feet. Not a good feeling, is it, Jim?"

Shimko narrowed his eyes and stared at me warily.

"I mean, it's depressing," I said. "You work all week long to make ends meet, get a couple days off to go deer hunting, and you see plenty of deer but no horns. I've been there myself, Jim. And before I became a game warden, I gotta admit there were times when I found myself in the same situation as you."

I paused for a moment, then shrugged casually. "I know what happened, Jim. And I understand. You were heading back to the truck after a long day's hunt when a doe walks out in front of you and stands there asking for it. I mean, what's a guy supposed to do?"

Shimko squinted at me guardedly.

"Happens all the time," I said, my voice laced with faux empathy. "Completely understandable."

"So," he said, "are you saying I'll get off with a warning if I admit I shot the doe that your deputy found?"

I shook my head. "No, Jim, but I will give you a break with only a single fine for shooting the deer. I won't prosecute you for hunting after hours, or wanton waste, or for running off like you did—that's called resisting inspection and carries a nine-hundred-dollar fine."

Shimko put his palms firmly on his knees and stared at me. "You wouldn't be playing Let's Make a Deal if you could prove I did anything, would you?"

"We have your rifle, Jim," I said. "It was recently fired. Liam's rifle was cold. You two were the only hunters in the field when the deer was shot. And you ran off when you saw Deputy Pierce. If you didn't do anything wrong, why did you run?"

"I don't know. Just got scared, that's all."

"Scared of what?"

Shimko slid back in his chair to put distance between us. "I don't want to talk to you anymore," he said. "I didn't want to be here tonight anyway but Liam made me come with him."

Realizing it was time for Plan B, I had Jeff bring Liam McCoy into the room and escort Shimko out of hearing range down the hallway.

"Jim told me he shot the doe," I said to Liam, hoping he'd believe me. "Too bad you didn't take Deputy Pierce's offer and come clean like Jim just did. I know Jeff well and he won't give you a second chance. He's a hard man. He'll write you up for a slew of poaching violations. Probably cost you thousands in fines."

Liam looked at me with alarm. "Thousands?" he asked.

"Yep. It's called aiding and abetting. Carries the same fine as if you'd shot the deer yourself. But I'm willing to speak to Jeff on your behalf, Liam. Get him to back off. But you need to tell me what happened tonight. If you do, I'll guarantee you won't be prosecuted."

"You can do that?"

"Jeff likes me," I said. "He doesn't like you, but he likes me. So, yes, I promise you won't be prosecuted if you cooperate."

Liam leaned back in his chair and mulled over my offer for a minute. "Fair enough," he said finally. "We were walking back to my truck when a doe came running across the field in front of us. Jim shot at it. I told him not to but he did it anyway. It was dark and we thought he missed, so we didn't bother looking for it. We were almost back to my truck when we saw Deputy Pierce. That's when Jim took off running."

I stood from my chair and walked to the doorway, signaling Jeff to bring Jim Shimko back.

"You're free to leave," I told Liam.

Jeff brought Shimko into the room and gestured for Liam to follow him outside. Both men exchanged tense glances as they passed.

I waited until Liam was out of earshot, then said, "Liam told me you shot the deer."

Shimko shook his head frantically. "He's crazy, man. I never fired my gun all day."

"You're lying, Jim. I told you before that we checked your gun. It had been recently fired."

He thought for a moment, eyes darting left and right. Then: "Hold it! Now I remember. I was having target practice earlier that day."

I was growing weary of Shimko's lame excuses. I intended to use Liam's admission against him in a court of law, hoping it would be enough for a conviction.

"You can go," I said to Shimko.

"What's gonna happen now?" he asked.

"I'm going to charge you with every game law violation I can think of, just like I told you before."

After guiding Shimko out of the police station, Jeff returned to the interrogation room with two Styrofoam cups of black coffee. He handed me a steaming cup, and I explained what had happened.

"We're going to need more proof," he said, "I know Liam McCoy. He'll change his story before he gets back to his uncle's tonight."

"I was afraid of that," I said. "I guess there's no chance of finding a bullet in the carcass."

"Gut shot," Jeff grunted. "That slug is long gone."

I nodded with disappointment.

"I'll tell you what," Jeff said. "Tomorrow at daybreak, I'll head back into the field to look for a spent shell from Shimko's rifle. With any luck, we might get a ballistics match."

As dawn broke over the horizon, Jeff Pierce slid out of his pickup truck and began his search. Dewdrops sparkled like tiny diamonds on the grass in the early light, the calm Sunday morning silence broken only by the occasional call of a distant crow.

The odds were against him, he knew. The chance of finding a bullet casing in the vast field of tangled weeds and hay-like grass was slim to none. But he'd faced improbable outcomes before as a deputy game warden and never let them hold him back.

As Jeff reached the spot where he'd found the gut-shot doe, he paced a hundred yards out and began circling the field. He moved deliberately, each step measured, his eyes scouring the ground cover. Soon, he spotted two distinct trails of flattened grass, etched by human footprints. The tracks emerged from the distant tree line and stretched toward the road where Liam had parked his truck the previous day. Jeff followed the imprints until one set veered off, then doubled back toward the road. Convinced this was where Shimko had broken away to take the shot at the deer, Jeff combed the ground cover. A sudden glint of sunlight caught his eye, reflecting off something nestled in the grass. He crouched low, parting the tall blades with care.

A gleaming .30-30 brass casing lay before him, winking in the light.

Jeff called Liam McCoy the next day and thanked him for admitting that Jim Shimko had shot the deer.

"I never said that!" insisted Liam. "I told Wasserman I didn't know who shot the deer."

"So you're saying Wasserman is lying?"

"I'm saying there's a misunderstanding, that's all. Besides, you didn't see anything, so you can't prove we did anything."

Jeff told him about the foot trail he'd discovered in the Thirty-Acre Field and the .30-30 casing he'd found.

"So what? That could have been anybody," Liam shot back.

"But it wasn't anybody," Jeff said. "It was you and Shimko. The trail led directly back to where your truck was parked. I could see where Shimko stopped to take a shot at the deer and where he turned and ran when he saw me."

"That's bogus, man. You're just trying to trap me, just like Wasserman last night."

"What I'm trying to do is get you off the hook for a big fine," Jeff said. "I'm still willing to do that but you'll need to start cooperating first."

Jeff could hear Liam's heavy breathing on the other end of the line.

"Last chance," Jeff warned. "I'm taking the casing and Shimko's rifle to the state police crime lab for a ballistics examination. They'll compare the mark on the primer with the rifle's firing pin. I believe they'll find a match."

Jeff had hoped that Liam would accept his final offer for a break. Instead, there was an audible *Click!* and the phone went dead.

The Pennsylvania State Police Crime Lab in Harrisburg is a 260-mile round-trip from Tunkhannock and is located across the street from the Pennsylvania Game Commission Training School. Since I was scheduled to teach a class on fur trapping for new cadets at the school in January, I waited until then to submit Shimko's rifle for a ballistics exam.

When the day finally arrived, I invited Jeff Pierce to ride along with me and he eagerly accepted. He welcomed the opportunity to visit the lab as well as the Game Commission's training facility.

Officially known as The Ross Leffler School of Conservation, the Training School has been the Game Commission's training facility for state game wardens since 1932. The school is part college and part police academy, with a training program of about fifty weeks. Cadets undergo more than a thousand hours of instruction covering over a hundred different subjects. Many of the instructors are veteran game wardens, and I was honored to be selected as one of the teachers for part of the day.

I was confident that the Crime Lab would match Shimko's rifle (which belonged to Liam's father) with the empty cartridge case Jeff found in the Thirty-Acre Field. Ballistics examiners can identify the weapons used in criminal acts by examining cartridge cases for markings left by the firing pin (also known as the striker) after the gun has been fired. Firing pin impressions are considered one of the most important toolmarks in ballistics. A specially designed microscope is used to examine the cartridge case to identify the markings. Just as no two human fingerprints are identical, no two firearms will leave the same impression on a cartridge case. When a match is found, it is considered indisputable evidence in trial courts across the nation.

Because the Crime Lab conducts hundreds of ballistics examinations each year, it would take months for me to be notified about the results. They say patience is a virtue, and this certainly holds true for game wardens as we work to unravel complicated poaching cases, advancing one step at a time.

The following spring, Jeff was hosting a family birthday party in his backyard when Liam's father, Fin McCoy, and two of his friends drove a pickup truck into his driveway, blowing the horn and shouting for him to come out front. Uncertain of their intentions, Jeff ushered all his guests inside the house. He concealed his duty weapon behind his back and instructed his wife, Pearl, to call the state police.

As Jeff walked out to confront the men, they climbed out of their truck and stood in his driveway. Fin McCoy was the biggest of the bunch, at six feet four inches and well over two hundred pounds. He lumbered toward Jeff in an uneven stagger. The others stood by his truck with cans of beer in their hands.

"Stop right there!" Jeff warned. They were about twenty feet apart.

Fin McCoy swayed from side to side and pointed a meaty index finger at Jeff. "You took my gun from my son," he croaked. "I want it back. You had no right to do that!"

"I had every right," Jeff said. "Your son's friend, Jim Shimko, used that rifle to shoot an illegal doe. I took it to the State Police Crime Lab for a ballistics exam. When they're through with it, you'll get it back."

Fin stared at Jeff for a moment, his expression a mix of confusion and resolve.

"I'd advise you and your friends to get off my property," Jeff warned. "You're all trespassing and I'm losing my patience real fast."

One of the men called from behind: "Come on, Fin. We'll stop at Dimitri's for another round of drinks. I'm getting thirsty and he ain't got your gun, anyway."

Fin McCoy spat on the ground and glared at Jeff. "You better make sure I get my gun back." Then he turned and trudged slowly back to his truck.

Jeff was relieved that McCoy wasn't sitting behind the steering wheel as they drove off.

T he crime lab results arrived several weeks later. As suspected, the .30-30 shell casing that Jeff found matched the rifle used by Shimko. Liam McCoy and Jim Shimko were notified about the evidence and were told that charges would be filed against both men: Shimko for shooting a doe in closed season and Liam for aiding and abetting in the unlawful hunt.

Shimko quickly confessed, stating that he didn't want his friend Liam to face charges for something he did alone. Regardless, both men had been given the chance to cooperate with us multiple times and refused. As a result, they were each charged with multiple Game Law violations in addition to killing a doe in closed season. Their fines soared into the thousands, and their hunting privileges were revoked for many years.

Danger Down the Sights.
~Book by Barney Berlinger

BAD IDEA

ONE BEAUTIFUL SATURDAY afternoon in November 1972, Ed Bond was patrolling along Route 413 in Bucks County when he noticed a hunter with a shotgun on his arm and an English setter working the field about seventy yards away.

He didn't see a hunting license displayed on the hunter's back, so he parked at the side of the road and walked out to speak with him.

The hunter was watching his setter work the field, oblivious to the warden behind him until his dog turned to investigate, prompting the hunter to turn as well.

"Get off my land!" the hunter shouted. "Game wardens aren't welcome here!"

Unmoved, Ed continued on, determined to find out why the man didn't have a license.

The hunter stomped across the field toward Ed, cursing and swearing like a madman. "Are you deaf?" he roared. "I told you to get off my land!"

Although his shotgun was pointed down as he advanced, it hadn't been unloaded and still posed a danger.

"Point your muzzle in the air and stay where you are," Ed commanded as he strode toward the man.

The hunter paused and stared at Ed, seemingly unable to comprehend why the game warden was issuing commands after being told to leave his property. His English setter sat obediently by his side, looking up at him with its head tilted as if questioning why they had stopped hunting.

Ed continued on until they were a few feet apart. In his sixties, the man wore a safety-orange ballcap and vest over khaki hunting pants. He had an oval head, stern gray eyes, and a bulbous nose lined with spidery veins.

"I didn't see a hunting license on your back," Ed said to him. "Where is it?"

"I don't need a hunting license on my own land," the hunter replied angrily. "Why don't you go pester somebody who actually deserves it?"

"I know who owns this land and it's not you," Ed told him. "Besides, only people who farm for a living can hunt without a license, and I know you're not one of them, either."

Ed paused, expecting a response, but the man just stood there, glaring at him.

"I want to see some identification," Ed directed.

"You're not a cop," he snorted. "I don't have to show you a thing."

Ed said, "If you don't show me a driver's license or some other official form of identification, I'll have no choice but to place you under arrest and take you to the nearest district court. I'm sure you don't want that."

Cursing under his breath, the man reached into his back pocket and pulled out a ragged leather wallet. He thrust out his arm, wallet in hand, and sneered at Ed. "Satisfied?"

"I don't want your wallet," Ed responded. "Open it and show me your ID."

Shaking his head in disdain, the man fished through his wallet until he found a driver's license. He pinched it between two stubby fingers and held it out.

Ed took the license and looked it over. The man's name was Harvey Timkin. He lived on a property that bordered the land he was hunting on.

Ed took a pen and notepad from his breast pocket and jotted down the information from his license.

"What are you doing that for?" Timkin grunted.

Ed glanced up at him. "I'm going to file a citation against you for hunting without a license.

More cursing and swearing.

"Calm down," Ed told him.

Timkin fumed. "I'm going to have your job," he shouted. "Just wait and see."

I'm going to have your job. The words just hung there. Ed thought about how many times he'd heard this same old tune from some overbearing, self-important windbag.

"Let me see if I understand what you're saying," Ed said. "You are going to have my job, for me doing my job by arresting you for hunting without a license. In the first place, you couldn't do my job. And in the second place, I'll give you the telephone number of the Division Office. You can call them and tell them that Ed Bond arrested you for hunting without a license and that you want his job. The supervisor is overworked and under a lot of stress, so he might enjoy a good laugh."

Timkin's face reddened, eyes bulging in their sockets, nostrils flaring like a rodeo bull. *"Who do you think you're talking to?"* he roared.

Ed heard a car door slam from behind. Then a second door. Timkin heard it too and glanced over Ed's shoulder toward the road. Ed watched as Timkin's expression transformed from raging fury to a mix of surprise and alarm. Then, without another word, Timkin spun on his heels and marched across the field away from Ed with his dog at his side.

More than a little reluctant to turn his back on Timkin while he still had a gun in his hands, Ed stood and watched until he was well out of shotgun range.

As Ed turned toward the road, he was surprised to see that two local farmers had stopped and parked their truck behind his car. One held a rifle in his hands. The sound of their doors slamming shut had been a clear warning for Timkin to back off, as he was being watched.

They were what you call good ole boys: the Brogan brothers, Frank and Steve. They farmed across Ed's patrol district and were on good terms with him. Because they suffered significant crop damage caused by deer, they always kept a rifle in their truck.

"Everything okay, Ed?" Frank Brogan asked as Ed stepped onto the road.

"Just fine," Ed said. "I think that might have had something to do with you two gentlemen."

Steve Brogan said, "We thought you might appreciate some company. We know that guy; he's a few bricks short of a full load."

"One sandwich short of a picnic," his brother Jim said with a breezy laugh.

Ed couldn't help smiling at their good humor despite their distaste for Harvey Timkin. And he knew that if Timkin had planned any violent behavior, the brothers would have done whatever was necessary to assist him.

In the end, as furious as Timkin was, he still paid his fine without taking a hearing, and Ed never heard from him again, even though he had threatened to "have his job."

Thinking back, Ed couldn't believe that all the fuss had been over a twenty-dollar fine and a hunting license that Timkin could have bought for just five bucks.

It is often said that when things start bad, they usually end bad, and today was to be one of those examples for Ed Bond.

With numerous hunters afield, hunting accidents are bound to occur from time to time. Ed had investigated many throughout his long career. Fortunately, most were not severe, involving only a few shotgun pellets that resulted in minor injuries to individuals.

Regardless of their severity, all incidents required investigation. Ed's job was to identify both the victim and the offender, establish the cause of the offense, and determine if any violations were committed. While it is an unpleasant task, piecing together a hunting accident can be intriguing. What caused it? How could it have been prevented? Did it occur by mere chance or develop out of sheer negligence?

Ed realized that hunting accidents are nearly always caused by negligence, which is often fueled by greed. Unfortunately, some hunters measure the success of a hunt solely by the kill. Otherwise, they reason, the day is a loss.

Hunters who feel they *must* shoot something, and if they come home empty-handed, they've somehow become a lesser person, can be dangerous not only to others but to themselves. The wise sportsman chooses his hunting companions carefully, avoiding those who are out to prove they're the best "hunter" in the county. People like this are often too quick to pull the trigger.

Contrary to common belief, hunting accidents are not always caused by novice hunters. Typically, they involve a man aged twenty-one to fifty who has hunted for most of his life and is using a shotgun for turkeys or small game when the incident occurs.

And so it was, a few hours after dealing with Harvey Timkin, that Ed noticed someone frantically blinking their headlights and honking behind him as he cruised along a rural back road.

Ed pulled over and a car stopped beside him. He was surprised to see his friend, Barney Berlinger, behind the wheel, his face lined with worry. In the passenger seat, a man in his fifties grimaced in pain while clutching a crudely bandaged, blood-soaked hand.

Berlinger leaned forward to speak through his open passenger window. "Ed, there's been an accident. We have to get to the hospital fast!"

Ed didn't wait to ask questions. He reached down and flipped a toggle switch, activating his emergency lights. Then he shifted his transmission into DRIVE and sped toward the main highway with Barney Berlinger trailing close behind.

While en route, Ed picked his mic off the dash and radioed a Game Commission dispatcher, directing him to notify Doylestown Hospital that he was bringing in a gunshot victim.

The hospital was a twenty-minute drive. They made it in ten. Ed screeched to a halt at the emergency room entrance and parked. Berlinger pulled up right behind him. Ed leaped out the door and rushed to Berlinger's car, where they carefully eased the injured man out. The man groaned, clutching his bandaged left hand as two orderlies and a nurse rushed over with a wheelchair and whisked him into the emergency room.

His name was William Westley. Ed wanted to interview him about the accident but knew he would be under medical supervision for some time. So after moving their vehicles to a parking lot, Ed and Barney went to the hospital cafeteria to grab a cup of coffee and discuss the incident.

Berlinger had a Regulated Hunting Grounds licensed by the Game Commission where pheasants were stocked for members who paid to hunt. He leaned back in his cafeteria chair, cradling a steaming coffee, and explained that William Westley had come by earlier to hunt.

"Accidents happen," Berlinger said, his tone heavy and somber. "But wait till you hear about this one."

It was a striking and colorful bird, its plumage iridescent in the early morning sun as William Westley drove his new Jeep Wagoneer onto the property and came to an abrupt stop. He couldn't believe his good fortune. Standing before him was a magnificent male pheasant, among the largest he'd ever seen. With its long tail, white-ringed neck and glossy feathers, it was a beautiful sight to behold.

Careful not to spook the bird, he eased open his door and slipped out clutching his English-made double-barrel twelve-gauge shotgun. Without taking his eyes off his prize, he stood behind his vehicle, broke open his shotgun, and reached into his vest pocket for two shells. Ever so slowly, he slipped the shells into the chamber by feel alone, then quietly closed the action and shouldered the gun.

Twenty yards away, the pheasant pecked at the gravel in the parking lot, oblivious of his presence.

Westley slid his index finger against the front trigger and slowly squeezed, expecting the shotgun to discharge and kick back into his shoulder. But there was only a thin, metallic click. Stunned and confused, he quickly pulled the second trigger.

Click!

He was unaware that he had accidentally dropped two smaller twenty-gauge shells into the barrels, which slid down and became lodged inside. The firing pins had fallen on empty spaces.

Thinking he'd dropped the shells on the ground and not wanting to take his eyes off the target, he quickly reloaded.

This time he got it right, with two twelve-gauge shells.

He'd just committed one of the worst mistakes of his life: never carry different gauge shotgun shells in your hunting coat. It could cost you your life.

When he pulled the trigger and the twelves hit the twenties, the gun barrel exploded, blowing part of his hand away with it.

Later that evening, Ed visited Westley in the hospital. After the usual, *Sorry this happened to you and how are you doing?* he informed him that he would have to complete a hunting accident report. However, under the circumstances, Ed filled out the information for him.

Ed couldn't help but recall the story of a big game hunter who shot a lion on an African safari. He didn't kill it, but wounded it just enough to infuriate the big cat. Enraged, the lion charged at a blistering fifty miles per hour, closing in fast.

The hunter thought, "No problem, I'll finish him off easily with my trusty .470 double-barrel rifle. I could drop an elephant with this baby."

He threw the gun to his shoulder when the lion was about thirty feet away and about to spring on our fearless nimrod.

But when he pulled the triggers, he heard the most dangerous sound one will ever hear when attempting to stop an enraged lion with revenge on its mind.

That sound is *click-click!*

Fortunately, his guide took matters into his own hands and finished the job for him.

*Something hidden. Go and find it. Go and look behind the Ranges—
Something lost behind the Ranges. Lost and waiting for you. Go!*
 ~Rudyard Kipling

HIDE AND SEEK
DECEMBER 1962

E<small>D</small> BOND WAS ON HIS WAY out the door, the chill of fresh snow crunching on his boots, when the call came in. It was buck season and his phone had been ringing off the hook all week. Thinking it might be another deer case, he walked back into his office and lifted the handset off the cradle. "Game Commission. Bond speaking…"

"Hello, this is Mrs. Stevenson." Her voice was soft yet urgent. "My daughters were sledding in the snow and found a dead deer back in the woods on our property. Could you please come and take it away?"

Ed asked for her address and told her he would head over to take a look. There were many deer in Bucks County. It could be just another roadkill or a deer shot by a hunter that had not been found. Either way, he was responsible for removing the carcass, just as he had done hundreds of times before in Bucks County.

The property was located in a more rural section of his district. A modest ranch house sat high on a hill surrounded by several acres of open meadow. Ed drove up the freshly plowed driveway and saw a woman standing by the open garage with two little girls at her side. The children waved at him as he topped the driveway and parked. The girls were twins who looked about ten years old. They wore identical red hooded snowsuits with brown insulated boots and woolen mittens. In her early thirties, their mother was dressed in a woolen white and black plaid coat, snow boots, and fashionable black leather gloves.

Ed shouldered open his door and walked over to them while zipping his coat against the icy breeze. Mrs. Stevenson was tall and slender with wavy brown hair and dark eyes.

"Thank you for coming," she said. "I'm Jenny, and these are my two daughters, Susie and Linda."

The girls stared at Ed with wide, innocent eyes. "We found a big deer when we were sledding," one said. The other nodded in harmony. They were identical.

"Can you show me where you found it?" Ed asked.

"Yes!" they sang out as one.

Ed looked at their mother for approval. She smiled and nodded her consent.

The twins were watching and their eyes sparkled with delight.

"Follow us!" one breathed eagerly.

"Come on!" the other quickly chimed in. And off they plodded side by side through the foot-deep snow with Ed trailing close behind.

The deer, a doe, lay just inside the tree line. It had been gutted and dragged several hundred feet downhill through the snow and hidden in a shallow washout. Whoever shot the illegal deer was attempting to conceal it. A single set of boot prints led from the carcass to a winding township road several hundred yards below. From his vantage point on the hill, Ed could see for a great distance. There were no vehicles parked anywhere. Although the poacher was long gone, Ed was confident he'd come back for his kill, most likely under the cover of darkness. He planned to be there when the poacher returned.

"Thanks for showing me the deer," Ed told the girls.

"I saw it first," said one.

"Did not!" declared the other.

"Did too."

"Did not."

Ed quickly cut in. "You both led me here," he said with a reassuring smile. "That's what's important because I never would have found the deer without your help."

The girls looked up at him and smiled contentedly, their cheeks rosy from the bitter cold.

"What's going to happen to the deer?" one asked.

"I'll take it to an orphanage where the children can have venison for dinner," Ed replied.

"What's venison?" they asked in unison.

"Deer meat," Ed said. "It's even better than hamburgers."

The twins looked at him with wonderment in their eyes. Then: *"Ewwwww!"* they cried.

Ed couldn't help but chuckle. "Come on, girls," he said. "Let's head on back; your mom will be waiting for us."

It was pitch black, and Ed had been standing in snow halfway up to his knees for hours waiting for the poacher to return. A large oak tree offered some protection from the wind. It was still bitterly cold, his every breath appearing as a condensation cloud.

High on the hill, he could see the road below. When headlights from a slow-moving vehicle finally appeared, his pulse quickened. But the motorist never stopped and Ed watched in dismay as the car vanished around a distant bend in the road.

Ed began to wonder how much longer he wanted to stay. His feet were blocks of ice. His hands were so cold that he wasn't sure he could effectively draw his revolver from its holster.

The longer he stood there, the colder he became. When the clouds began to part, revealing a bright full moon that set the snowy landscape ablaze, it almost looked like dawn was breaking. With it, the temperature began to drop even more.

For some reason, aside from it being December, perhaps, the famous poem *The Night Before Christmas* came to mind, particularly the line: *The moon on the breast of the new fallen snow gave the luster of midday to objects below.* Tonight, the object bathed in that silvery glow was Ed Bond. Shivering, he decided to leave the deer and return for it later. His teeth chattered so loudly he feared they'd probably reveal his position to the poacher if he came by, anyway.

When Ed returned the following day, the temperature had soared into the mid-forties under a brilliant sun. Expecting to find the deer still there, he was surprised and disappointed to discover it was gone. Fresh bootprints and a swath in the snow revealed that the poacher had dragged the carcass downhill to the road and loaded it into a vehicle.

Because the deer was killed several hundred yards from the road, high on a hill on private property, Ed felt sure that the poacher lived in the immediate area. There was a house along the road a short distance away. He decided to pay the folks a visit.

A wood-frame two-story colonial, it had recently been given a fresh coat of brown stain. The front door and shutters were an attractive shade of red, and the roof appeared to have been recently replaced. The home was well kept, the driveway plowed clear of snow, and the outbuildings, old as they were, looked to be in good repair.

Ed parked in the driveway and walked up to the front door and knocked. When no one answered, he went to the backyard to see if anyone was around.

The snow-covered yard was littered with footprints, some leading to an open storage shed a short distance away. Ed went to the shed and looked inside. He saw a John Deere riding lawn mower and some farm tools scattered about but there was no deer.

On the way back to his car, he noticed the rusted hood of an old pickup truck propped against the house. A sheen of water gleamed on its flat surface, which seemed out of place. Ed went over for a closer look. The hood, he realized, had recently been moved—likely from a snow-covered spot elsewhere. The late morning sun had melted the snow off the hood, leaving a slick of water that drew his attention. Someone had placed it there within the last few hours. But why?

Curious, he eased the hood back from the wall and discovered a small wooden crate behind it. Inside the crate were the heads and hides of two recently killed antlerless deer.

Ed was certain that one of the deer was the doe he'd kept watch over for hours before. The other one might also have been killed nearby. Both had been taken in closed season. A clear violation. Determined, he went directly to the JP's office and secured a search warrant for the house and surrounding property.

When Ed returned a few hours later, he saw a Dodge pickup truck parked in the driveway. He pulled in behind it and parked, then stepped up on the front porch and knocked. He could hear a television in the background, indicating someone might be home.

Footfalls were coming, and Ed recognized the man when the door opened moments later. His name was Perry Toth. Ed had caught him with an illegal roadkilled deer two years ago.

Toth was in his fifties with brown hair slicked back and a thin, angular face. He wore a tan flannel shirt untucked over creased blue jeans. "Warden Bond?" he said, his eyes blinking with unease. "Can I help you?"

"I'm investigating a tip about a doe that was killed yesterday," Ed said. "Thought you might've heard a shot or seen something that could help me."

Toth slowly shook his head. "Sorry, but I haven't seen anything unusual."

"Are you aware of any hunting activity in the area?"

"My son killed a deer behind the house during archery season," he said. "Nobody has been hunting around here since." He paused, then said, "Look, I was just about to prepare dinner, so if there's nothing else…"

"There is," Ed said as he pulled his search warrant from an inside coat pocket. He handed it to Toth.

"What's this?" Toth asked, glancing at the warrant and then back at Ed.

"Exactly what it says. It's a search warrant for your house and every building on your property."

"But why? What are you looking for?"

"Unlawfully killed deer, or any venison that's in your freezer or on your property."

Toth swallowed hard. He stepped back and motioned for Ed to come inside. "Follow me," he said. "I'll show you what I have."

As Ed trailed Toth into the kitchen, he saw a teenage girl in a green and white high school uniform watching them from a balcony. She quickly vanished when he met her eyes.

Perry Toth opened the freezer and pulled out a package of deer meat. "This is all that's left of the deer my son killed in October," he said. "It was a legal buck."

"That's not what I'm here for, and I think you know it," Ed said. "You can start cooperating and show me where you have the deer, or I'll go through your entire house, room by room, until I find it."

Toth closed his eyes and sighed. "I don't want you to do that."

"Then tell me where you have the deer."

"You're right," he said, his tone somber. "It's down in the basement. Come on, I'll show you."

Ed followed Toth as he opened the cellar door, flicked on the light switch and walked down the steps. When they reached the bottom, Ed saw the skinned and quartered carcass of a deer soaking in a tub of saltwater.

"It's a doe," Toth admitted. "Tell me what the fine is and I'll pay. But first, I have to pick up my daughter from the school bus down the road."

"How many children do you have?" Ed asked.

"Just one."

"I'll have to go with you."

Toth squinted at him. "What for?"

"Because I'm not finished with my investigation."

What Toth really wanted to do was hurry over to his friend's house and warn him that the game warden was hot on his trail.

Ed played along and followed Toth back up the cellar steps and out the front door as if he believed the story about picking up his daughter at the bus—the same daughter he had seen on the balcony minutes before.

"I want you to come over to my car before we go any further," Ed said, motioning for him to follow.

The two men walked to the back of Ed's car and faced each other.

"I know your daughter isn't on any school bus," Ed told him. "I saw her standing on the balcony when I followed you into the kitchen."

Toth looked wounded. He said nothing.

"You've lied to me twice now," Ed cautioned. "But I'm willing to overlook those lies and work with you if you promise not to lie anymore."

Toth looked over Ed's shoulder into the middle distance. Then he met his eyes and nodded. "Okay. I promise, no lies."

Ed asked, "Is the deer in your basement the only one that was killed, or are there others?"

"That's the only one," Toth said.

Ed dug into his coat pocket, pulled out his car keys, and unlocked his trunk.

Toth froze when he saw the wooden crate containing the heads and hides of two deer. Then his eyes welled with tears and he started to weep.

Ed couldn't help but feel a pang of sympathy for the man. He closed the trunk and told him that nothing was going to happen to him, no one was going to hurt him, he was not going to jail, and he would simply have to pay a fine as long as he told him who else was involved.

Toth nodded that he understood and wiped the tears from his face with his sleeve.

"I can't go through this anymore," he whimpered pitifully. "It's too stressful and it's just not worth it. The other people involved were my son Carson, Harold Perkins, and Teddie Metz...."

After getting directions to Harold Perkins' place, Ed put Toth's warrant in the breast pocket of his uniform with only the words, *Commonwealth of Pennsylvania Search Warrant* visible. He then drove to Perkins' house.

When Ed knocked, a large man in his forties stepped outside into the cold and closed the door behind him. He wore grease-stained jeans and a sleeveless gray T-shirt that only partially covered the dense black hair on his chest.

"Game warden?" he said, his forehead furrowed in mock confusion. "Can I help you with something?"

"I think you know why I'm here," Ed responded.

Perkins' eyes fell on the search warrant protruding from Ed's top pocket.

Ed said, "I just left Perry Toth's house. He told me all about the deer you two killed. The heads and hides are in the trunk of my car. One of them belongs to you."

Perkins looked at Ed's sedan parked in the street, then back to Ed. "Perry ratted on me, huh?" he said, shaking his head with regret. "Guess I shouldn't be surprised. He always was a gutless wonder."

"I have a search warrant," bluffed Ed. "If you don't want me rummaging through your house, you should show me where you have the deer."

Perkins stared down at the ground and nodded as if deep in thought. A curtain flickered in the window behind him.

"How many people are inside?" Ed asked.

Perkins looked up suddenly. "Just my wife and a friend of mine. Why?"

Ed shrugged. "Thought I saw someone at the window." He paused for a moment, then said, "Look, I'm not going anywhere without the deer, so why don't we just get this over with?"

Perkins blew a weary sigh. "You're right," he said. Then he turned and opened the front door. "The deer is hanging in my basement."

Ed followed Perkins into the living room, where a portly man in his thirties relaxed in a polyester lounge chair watching football on TV. A woman sat stiffly on the couch next to him, her hands flat on her lap. Neither of them looked up as Ed and Harold Perkins walked by on their way to the basement.

They descended the steps expecting to find a deer carcass, but when they reached the bottom, they saw an empty skinning gambrel.

"Is this some kind of a joke?" Ed asked sourly.

Perkins shook his head. "I swear the deer was right here." He looked up at the top of the steps and set his jaw. A tell.

Ed strode back up the cellar steps and over to the man in the lounge chair, blocking his view of the TV. "You're Teddie Metz, aren't you?" he said.

"Yep, that was my name the last time I checked."

"Where's the deer?"

Metz rolled his eyes and looked away.

"You're in enough trouble already," Ed said. "Unless you want interference with a state officer added to your charges."

"It was his idea!" Mrs. Perkins burst out suddenly. "He hid it behind the couch!"

Ed looked behind the couch and saw the deer carcass lying on the wooden floor.

He turned and faced Teddie Metz. "You put it there; now pick it up and take it to my car. I'm confiscating it."

Metz offered Ed a dopey smile, then he struggled off the lounge chair, walked over to the carcass, and hoisted it onto his broad shoulders with a grunt.

"You got it, boss," he said. Then he carried the deer out the door, with Ed Bond and Harold Perkins following closely behind him.

As Ed tied the carcass to his deer rack, Perry Toth and his son arrived in Toth's Dodge pickup and parked behind him. Ed called everyone together, and they all agreed to meet at the JP's office to settle the case.

The fines for all four men totaled $800 (equivalent to $8000.00 today). When Judge Granger read the charges to the defendants, they all pleaded guilty except Toth's son, Carson, who admitted that he knew about the deer but claimed he hadn't assisted the others in any way.

When Judge Granger asked him if he knew the deer were illegal, he said, "Well, yeah." The judge then asked him if he had called the game warden. He replied, "Well, no." To which the judge replied, "That makes you an accessory before and after the fact...GUILTY!"

Note from Ed Bond

I am now 92 years old, and looking back I realize that I successfully solved and prosecuted this case—and many others—not because I was a master detective, but with a lot of help from the Almighty, a bit of luck, and the fact that I was dealing with basically decent people who simply took a chance and got caught.

Acknowledgments

I would like to thank the game wardens, who graciously consented to my use of their true accounts from their days afield.

Game Warden Ed Bond for his memories of days gone by.
Game Warden Jason Farabaugh for *The Keeper's Closet.*
Game Warden Jesse Cunningham for *A Shot in the Dark.*
Game Warden Rebecca Wolfe for *The Best-Laid Plans.*
Game Warden Jeff Pierce for *Gut Shot.*

My invaluable first readers were Maryann Wasserman and John Wasserman.

A special thanks to John Wasserman for the cover of this book and all the others over the years.

William Wasserman, a world champion third-degree black belt in the Korean martial art of *Tang Soo Do* and a former national bodybuilding champion, has written sixteen books about his life as a state game warden. He has received numerous awards for his work in wildlife conservation, including the United Bowhunters of Pennsylvania Game Protector of the Year Award, the Pennsylvania Game Commission's Northeast Region Outstanding Wildlife Conservation Officer Award, the National Society Daughters of the American Revolution Conservation Medal, and the Pennsylvania Trappers Association Presidential Award. Wasserman has been published in several national magazines, including *Black Belt, Pennsylvania Game News, Fur-Fish-Game, South Carolina Wildlife, International Game Warden,* and *The Alberta Game Warden.* Wasserman retired from the Pennsylvania Game Commission after thirty-two years of dedicated service and lives in South Carolina with his wife, Maryann.

www.ingramcontent.com/pod-product-compliance
Lightning Source LLC
Chambersburg PA
CBHW060504030426
42337CB00015B/1739